LIGHT IN MY DARKNESS

Light in My Darkness

HELEN KELLER

Revised and expanded by Ray Silverman
Foreword by Dorothy Herrmann

**SWEDENBORG
FOUNDATION**
West Chester, Pennsylvania

Library of Congress Cataloging-in-Publication Data

Keller, Helen, 1880–1968.
    Light in my darkness / Helen Keller ; revised and edited by Ray Silverman ; foreword by Dorothy Herrmann.—2nd ed., rev. and enl.
      p.   cm.
    Rev. ed. of: My religion. 1960.
    ISBN 0-87785-398-5
      1. New Jerusalem Church. 2. Swedenborg, Emanuel, 1688–1772.
    3. Keller, Helen, 1880–1968—Religion. 4. Swedenborgians—Biography.
    I. Silverman, Ray. II. Keller, Helen, 1880–1968. My religion. III. Title.
    BX8721.K35 2000
    289'.4'092—dc21
    [B]
                                                            99-059981

Cover and interior designed by Karen Connor
Edited by Stuart Shotwell

Cover image: Head and shoulder portrait of Helen age 40. Courtesy of the American Foundation for the Blind, Helen Keller Archives.

Manufactured in the United States of America

Swedenborg Foundation
320 North Church Street
West Chester, PA 19380
www.swedenborg.com

CONTENTS

ILLUSTRATIONS

Helen Keller in 1950, age 70. Reproduced by permission of Oscar White Archives, Pearl River, New York. PAGE ii

That word "water" dropped into my mind like the sun in a frozen winter world. The pump in the Keller backyard in Tuscumbia, Alabama, where Helen learned to sign her first word, "water." Reproduced by permission of the American Foundation for the Blind (AFB), Helen Keller Archives, New York. PAGE 4

One of the noblest champions true Christianity has ever known. Emanuel Swedenborg in his nineteenth year, circa 1707, unidentified artist. Courtesy of Adolph Stroh. PAGE 35

He was the Herald of a new dispensation. Swedenborg, with *Apocalypse Revealed*, by Pehr Krafft, the Elder. Swedenborg Image Archives. PAGE 44

All things upon earth represent and image forth all the realities of another world. Helen as a young woman, circa 1903. (AFB) PAGE 48

All are born for heaven, as the seed is born to become a flower and the little thrush in the nest is intended to become a song-bird. Helen with Alexander Graham Bell, 1901. (AFB) PAGE 73

All human beings live both in this natural world and in the spiritual realm at the same time. Helen with the inscription "God is Light." (AFB) PAGE 85

For a life in the dark, love is the surest guide. Helen with Anne Sullivan, circa 1894. Reproduced with permission of Perkins School for the Blind (PSB), Watertown, Massachusetts. PAGE 92

The joy of surmounting obstacles that once seemed unremovable . . . what other joy is there like it? Helen with the Martha Graham Dancers, circa 1954. (AFB) PAGE 106

In every limitation we overcome, and in the higher ideals we thus attain, the whole kingdom of love and wisdom is present. Helen Keller. Painting by Everett Raymond Kinstler. Reproduced with permission of Harvard Club of New York City. PAGE 118

There is no such thing as "otherworldliness" when we are convinced that heaven is not beyond us but within us. Helen as a young woman, circa 1904. PAGE 123

It was his mission to teach people to listen to the inward voice rather than to opinions and disputations. Swedenborg at his writing desk, by Torsten Schonberg. PAGE 132

Immured by silence and darkness, I possess the light that will give me vision a thousandfold—when death sets me free. Helen with her Braille Bible, circa 1961–63. (PSB) PAGE 140

Life is either a daring adventure or it is nothing. Helen on a ship near the Orkney Islands, circa 1932. (AFB) PAGE 151

FOREWORD TO
My Religion (1960)

IF A WORLDWIDE POLL WERE TO BE TAKEN TO DETERMINE THE most outstanding woman of our generation, no doubt the top selection would be Helen Keller.

The good she has done through her work for the blind and other handicapped people throughout the world is enormous. And many a person, with or without handicaps, has been inspired by Helen Keller's books.

One of the most helpful of these books is *My Religion*, in which she tells of her early problems and how she gained the inner resources to overcome her own handicaps and lead such a magnificent and noble life.

Miss Keller's dynamic personality shines out through her lovely paean of praise to God and her appreciation of the people who helped her spiritually, particularly a kindly old man who assisted Alexander Graham Bell in his work for the deaf and at the same time shared with Helen Keller the writings of the famous Swedish theologian Emanuel Swedenborg.

He was the Consul-General for Switzerland in the United States, Mr. John Hitz, and his service beyond the call of duty brought Helen Keller the great glow of Christian faith that shone through her life so splendidly! To read *My Religion* is a rich blessing that I wish every person might enjoy.

I am very glad to add my tribute to the many she has so deservedly received.

— NORMAN VINCENT PEALE

FOREWORD

As Helen Keller's biographer, I could not help noting that it was my subject's enduring belief in Swedenborgianism that enabled her to surmount the limitations of her complete deaf-blindness. From the beginning, she faced tragedies that would have crushed a less spiritual, less courageous woman.

Helen Adams Keller was born a normal, hearing-sighted infant, on June 27, 1880, in Tuscumbia, a small rural town in northwestern Alabama. For almost two halcyon years, her childhood was like most other people's. Then, in February 1882, when Helen was nineteen months old, she developed a severe congestion of the stomach and brain. The nature of her ailment, which was called "brain fever" by the doctors of the period, remains a mystery to this day. Some modern doctors believe it was scarlet fever, a contagious disease that is caused by a hemolytic streptococcus, while others are of the opinion that her symptoms were more indicative of meningitis, an inflammation of the delicate membranes that cover the spinal cord and brain. In any event, for several days the family doctor thought she would die. But the fever gradually subsided, and the child fell into a deceptively quiet sleep.

Believing their little daughter cured, the Kellers rejoiced. Only when Kate Keller, Helen's mother, passed her hand before the baby's eyes and they did not close and she rang a dinner bell and Helen did not respond did they realize that the illness had left her deaf, blind, and mute. She was living in a world where there was neither light nor sound. Medical tests would later reveal that she could perceive neither light nor objects and that she was completely deaf, possessing neither bone nor air conduction in either ear.

Through her unquenchable zest for life and learning, and with the help of her fiercely devoted teacher Annie Sullivan, Helen was able to transcend her severe disabilities. On April 5, 1887, at the well pump outside Ivy Green, Helen's childhood home in Tuscumbia, Annie Sullivan made the violent, intractable child hold her mug under the spout while she pumped. As the cold water gushed forth, filling the mug, she spelled "w-a-t-e-r" in Helen's free hand. Later, describing the experience to a friend, Annie wrote: "The word coming so close upon the sensation of cold water rushing over her hand seemed to startle her. She dropped the mug and stood as one transfixed. A new light came into her face. She spelled 'water' several times. Then she dropped on the ground and asked for its name and pointed to the pump and the trellis, and suddenly turning round she asked for my name. I spelled 'Teacher.'"

On that day, Helen's "soul was set free," as she later exultantly described the experience of grasping the idea of language.

Another spiritual liberation came to Helen when, as a young woman, she met the Swiss-born John Hitz, who was the secretary of Alexander Graham Bell, the famous American inventor of the telephone. An elderly, gentle man with a flowing beard, Hitz became her spiritual guardian, introducing her to the writings of Emanuel Swedenborg, the illustrious eighteenth-century Swedish theologian, scientist, and philosopher. Deeply moved by Swedenborg's accounts of the mystical visions he had experienced during his spiritual crisis when he turned away from scientific research and devoted himself to biblical study and the writing of religious philosophy, Helen became a devout Swedenborgian.

Swedenborg's *Heaven and Hell* was the first book of the philosopher's writings that Hitz gave to Helen in raised print. "I opened the big book, and lo, my fingers lighted upon a paragraph in the preface about a blind woman whose darkness was illumined with beautiful truths from Swedenborg's writings," Helen later wrote, observing that, as she read Swedenborg's words, she came to believe that his writings compensated her for the complete loss of her vision. From that moment on, never did she doubt that there was a spiritual body within her own imperfect physical one and that, after a few dark soundless years, the spiritual eyes within her own unseeing eyes would open to a world infinitely more satisfying than this flawed one:

> My heart gave a joyous bound. Here was a faith that emphasized what I felt so keenly—the separateness between soul and body, between a realm I could picture as a whole and the chaos of fragmentary things and irrational contingencies which my limited physical senses

met at every turn. I let myself go, as healthy, happy
youth will, and tried to puzzle out the long words and
the weighty thoughts of the Swedish sage.

Every morning before breakfast, Hitz laboriously transcribed
Swedenborg's writing into Braille for Helen to further her religious study. As Helen later commented, she credited Swedenborg with imparting to her "a richer interpretation of the Bible, a
deeper understanding of the meaning of Christianity and a precious sense of the Divine Presence in the world. . . . His central
doctrine is simple. It consists of three main ideas: God as Divine
Love, God as Divine Wisdom, and God as Power for use."

Thus, from the age of sixteen, Helen Keller considered herself
a Swedenborgian.

In the summer of 1896, Captain Keller died suddenly in Tuscumbia. Immediately, on learning of her father's demise, Helen
pleaded with Annie Sullivan, whom she always referred to as
"Teacher," to travel to Tuscumbia to be with her family. But Kate
Keller refused to let her daughter attend the funeral, making the
feeble excuse that the intense heat and humidity of Alabama in
the late summer would be bad for her health.

As Annie Sullivan spelled her mother's decision into her hand,
Helen began to sob. Not only was her father dead, but her family was refusing to let her share their grief. She felt more lonely
and isolated than ever. "He died last Saturday at my home in Tuscumbia," she later wrote a friend, "and I was not there. My own
loving father! Oh, dear friend, how shall I ever bear it."

Helen's only solace was in her newly discovered religion. She
wrote to Hitz:

Teacher has read "The Immortal Fountain" to me, and as she spelled the words into my hand, I forgot my heartache, and only thought of dear father in his heavenly home, surrounded by angels, and learning all that he could not learn here. So you see, what a great help these truths are to me. Oh, I have never needed them so sorely before.

Helen's first instruction in religion had come at age eight, fewer than two years after she had first grasped the idea of language. She had thought it a joke when an aunt had informed her that she was made of "dust," that God was her father, that God was love, and that God was everywhere. A nonbeliever, Annie Sullivan was hard pressed to answer Helen's questions, many of which Annie felt were unanswerable.

In embracing Swedenborgianism as her faith, Helen broke with her family's religious traditions. Her father was a Presbyterian who was active in the church, while her mother was an Episcopalian. Helen herself had received religious instruction from the illustrious Bishop Phillips Brooks at Trinity Church in Boston, Massachusetts, but she had lingering spiritual doubts about the relationship between divine love and the material world.

A highly educated woman who knew several languages, Helen graduated in 1904 from Radcliffe College, the first deaf-blind woman to graduate from college. An accomplished writer, she loved to read, often finding both illumination and escape in the rich world of her Braille books. As her nimble fingers skimmed the raised letters, she was unencumbered by blindness and deafness and could explore the myriad wonders of the universe.

But of all the books she read in college with her fingers, the philosophical treatises were the ones she most treasured:

> I was so happily at home in philosophy, it alone would have rendered those four difficult years worth while. . . . Philosophy taught me how to keep on guard against the misconceptions which spring from the limited experience of one who lives in a world without color and without sound. . . . I was delighted to have my faith confirmed that I could go beyond the broken arc of my senses and behold the invisible in the fullness of the light, and hear divine symphonies in silence. I had a joyous certainty that deafness and blindness were not an essential part of my existence, since they were not in any way a part of my immortal mind.

Of the philosophers, Emanuel Swedenborg remained her favorite. The famous Swedish member of Parliament and scientist was fifty-five years old when he had a series of profound religious experiences and abandoned his brilliant work in engineering, physics, and physiological science that anticipated many later discoveries. Before his illumination, he revealed that he had been instructed by dreams and experienced extraordinary visions. According to Swedenborg's own account, the Lord filled him with his divine spirit and sent Swedenborg to teach the doctrines of the New Church—the church meant by the "New Jerusalem" in the book of Revelation. He further testified that all this took place while he was reading the Bible, adding "For this purpose the Lord has opened the inner faculties of my mind and spirit, and has made it possible for me to be in the spiritual world with angels and at the same time in the natural world with

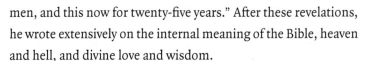

men, and this now for twenty-five years." After these revelations, he wrote extensively on the internal meaning of the Bible, heaven and hell, and divine love and wisdom.

Swedenborgianism, with its concepts of a universal spiritual reality and brotherhood, a loving God, and an afterlife in which no one would suffer from limitations and handicaps appealed to Helen. She drew much inspiration and insight from the Swedish seer's writings and his enthralling presentation of morality, calling them "the light in my darkness, the voice in my silence." According to Swedenborg, death is simply a transition to a new world, a larger, nobler life beyond the grave, and she believed that, in this spiritual world, she would not only be able to see and hear, but also could marry and enjoy the "conjugial love" that had been denied her in life.

"I am always eager to learn more about the spiritual world," she wrote to Hitz, explaining why the religion to which he had introduced her at age sixteen had become one of the sources of her strength:

> Swedenborgianism is more satisfying to me than the creeds about which I have read. For the very reason that it is the most spiritual and idealistic religion, it best supplies my peculiar needs. It makes me feel as if I had been restored to equality with those who have all their faculties. . . . I feel weary of groping, always groping along the darkened path that seems endless. At such times the desire for the freedom and the larger life of those around me is almost agonizing. But when I remember the truths you have brought within my reach, I am strong again and full of joy. I am no lon-

ger deaf and blind; for with my spirit I see the glory of
the all-perfect that lies beyond the physical sight and
hear the triumphant song of love which transcends the
tumult of this world. What appears to be my affliction
is due to the obscurity, yeah, the darkness, as Swedenborg says, occasioned by terrestrial things. I cannot
help laughing sometimes at the arrogance of those who
think they alone possess the earth because they have
eyes and ears. In reality, they see only shadows and
know only in part. They little dream that the soul is the
only reality, the life, the power which makes harmony
out of discord, completeness out of incompleteness.

In late March 1908, when Helen and her mother visited Washington, D.C., John Hitz met them at the railroad station. He
appeared in good health, putting his arm around her and spelling into her hand some affectionate German words of greeting,
his custom upon meeting her. After walking with them a short
distance, Hitz became weak and had trouble breathing. An
ambulance was summoned, but he died en route to a hospital.
When Helen, who was following in a carriage with her mother,
learned of her friend's death, her first reaction was that she must
be taken to the hospital room where his body was lying. After
passing her sensitive fingers over his face, which she had adored
but never seen, she kissed him goodbye for the last time. Later,
she wrote that she "could not have borne the loss of such an intimate and tender friend if I had thought he was indeed dead. But
his noble philosophy and certainty of the life to come braced me
with an unwavering faith that we should meet again in a world
happier and more beautiful than anything of my dreaming."

In the early 1920s, when she was almost forty years old, Helen Keller went on the vaudeville stage to support herself and her beloved teacher. She was a trouper, and not even the death of her mother Kate Keller in 1921, when she and Annie were appearing on the Orpheum circuit in Los Angeles, could prevent her from going onstage. "Every fiber of my being cried out at the thought of facing the audience, but it had to be done," she recalled. She had received the news of the death of her mother, whom she had not even known was seriously ill, only two hours before a performance.

Mrs. Keller had a lifelong dread of a prolonged terminal illness, and Helen took solace in the thought that her mother's death before she became completely incapacitated was what she had wished. But it was her own firm belief in Swedenborgianism and immortality that made it possible for her to bear the loss of her mother:

> I had absolute faith that we should meet again in the Land of Eternal Beauty; but oh, the dreary blank her going left in my life! . . . She seemed to have died a second time when I visited my sister in Montgomery the following April. The only thought that upheld me was that in the Great Beyond where all truth shines revealed she would find in my limitations a satisfying sense of God's purpose of good which runs like a thread of gold through all things.

With her mother dead, Helen now had only Annie Sullivan; but in 1921, while they were performing in Toronto, her devoted teacher collapsed with a severe case of the flu. In the ensuing years, Annie would be plagued by ill health. Not only was she fast approaching blindness, but she also suffered from numerous other ailments.

Helen's faith was again sorely tested when Annie Sullivan died in 1936. They had been together for nearly fifty years. People had been aware of Helen's dependence on Annie and wondered how she would be able to survive without her. But Helen was able to meet her severest crisis with immense courage and fortitude. "I ache all over as I remember how she grew thinner and thinner," Helen later recorded in the journal. Describing her own agony as a "Gethsemane I passed through" when Annie Sullivan passed away, Helen also wrote about the inner strength that came to her in the midst of this great sorrow:

> When she breathed no more, somehow the faith she had wished she could hold with me rose up stronger than ever and, leaning over, I said, "You know, dearest, don't you that life is beginning over again, glorious with light and peace." . . . There was such a surge of memories sweeping over me, and I remembered the first joyous days of release when we spelled winged words to each other, and life was a continuous great discovery.

In Helen Keller's view, modern medicine had made the last years of life bearable, while Swedenborgianism made heaven a place where all human beings would be given a second chance to be reunited with loved ones and she would be able to see and hear, as well as be reunited with Annie Sullivan. "The belief in immortality is in her bloodstream, as much a part of her as the red corpuscles," a friend noted. And in her tribute to Swedenborg, Helen wrote, "When I think of all those who would rejoice to have colorful details of that unseen world to which their loved ones have gone, the sacred responsibility of satisfying their doubting hearts is obvious."

Helen's immense vitality amazed and touched everyone who knew her, and in part, it was derived from her strong religious faith. When Helen "felt" a dance that the legendary dancer Martha Graham had choreographed especially for her, Graham observed: "She allows no ego block—lets nothing stand in the way; becomes a completely receptive instrument, a witness of God." Later she communicated to Helen through Polly Thomson, Helen's companion after the death of Annie Sullivan, that Helen was a great actress because she had love. In Graham's opinion, no one could be an inspired actress without it.

Indeed, for many persons, meeting Helen Keller was like having a religious experience. It was like an encounter with an angel. And almost invariably people were moved to tears. People, when they met her, were quick to point out her spiritual beauty, comparing her to a religious figure.

But, as I was to discover for myself in researching my biography of her, Helen Keller never considered herself an angel. She loved to laugh and to have people spell jokes into her hand; she loved stylish clothes, especially red high heels; and she also enjoyed a cocktail or two in the evening. Physically, she was a tall, beautiful woman, with regular, almost perfect features. In her youth, she had a luxuriant mane of chestnut hair that cascaded down her back. She had a lovely figure, but because of her deaf-blindness, her physical attributes, which were considerable, were usually not mentioned.

In June 1955, a week before her seventy-fifth birthday, Helen received an honorary degree from Harvard University, the first woman to be so honored. When her name was called, the entire audience rose for a standing ovation. She had never looked more beautiful—she was dressed entirely in white, with a white hat with small green flowers. Pinned to her dress was a corsage of white gardenias that the Swedenborgians had sent her. It was a measure of her respect and devotion to the New Church that she chose to wear these lovely flowers on this very special day of her life.

In later life, Helen read the Bible every morning, usually the Psalms. Her favorites were the ninetieth, the ninety-eighth, the hundredth, and of course, the twenty-third. As she once wrote:

> I confess I get rather exasperated with ministers who think there must be a special form to one's prayers, one way of approaching God. My feeling is that all prayers should spring from the Lord's prayer—after that I pray to God that I may act according to His law of life and to practice what I think and believe, not in words merely, but in acts. I really feel that there is a special bond between all earnest believers—Christians, Jews, Muslims—often I thank Him for permitting me to feel so close to Him.

Every Sunday, Helen celebrated her religion privately at her home, but even her closest friends did not know the nature of the service. It is certain, however, that it included Swedenborg's religious writings, which she said "have brought down to me truths from heaven that have given my spirit a thousand wings."

Helen Adams Keller died on Saturday afternoon, June 1, 1968, at her home, Arcan Ridge, near Westport, Connecticut. She had lived almost her entire life in gray silence and comprehended the world by the manual finger language, Braille, and lip-reading as well as by her senses of smell, taste, and touch. It was a few weeks before her eighty-eighth birthday. A few days earlier she had suffered a heart attack. Winnie Corbally, her companion at the time, was at her bedside when she died. The woman who had never feared death "drifted off in her sleep. She died gently," Winnie later said.

Helen had arranged for a Swedenborgian minister of the New Church in New York to officiate at her own funeral service in Westport, Connecticut. But this ceremony never took place, although the Swedenborgians later held their own memorial service for Helen in New York, which, according to one person who attended it, was beautiful and affecting.

Although Helen had been a devout Swedenborgian for most of her life, her family and trustees disregarded her wishes about their participation at her funeral. Four years before his sister's death, Phillips Keller, Helen's brother, had written Winnie Corbally that he and his wife wanted a prominent Presbyterian minister to conduct the funeral service for Helen at the Congregational Church in Westport. "The Kellers all started out as Presbyterians and Sister Mildred [Helen's younger sister], her daughter and their families [sic] are all life-long Presbyterians."

The service for Helen in Connecticut was canceled, and instead a funeral service was held in Washington, D.C., at the National Cathedral, where Woodrow Wilson was buried. Twelve hundred mourners, led by Chief Justice of the United States and Mrs. Earl Warren, honored Helen's memory in a nondenominational service.

Later, in a private interment in the columbarium of the Chapel of St. Joseph of Arimathea, the urn containing Helen's ashes was deposited next to those of Annie Sullivan and Polly Thomson. Ever since Annie's demise thirty-two years before, Helen had been convinced that, at the moment of her own death, she would see her teacher again. "What is so sweet as to awake from a troubled dream and behold a beloved face smiling upon you? I have to believe that such shall be our awakening from earth to heaven," she had written in *My Religion*.

Her belief in Swedenborgianism had released her from the fear of physical dissolution.

> I cannot understand why anyone should fear death. Life here is more cruel than death—life divides and estranges, while death, which at heart is life eternal, reunites and reconciles. I believe that when the eyes within my physical eyes shall open upon the world to come, I shall simply be consciously living in the country of my heart.

— DOROTHY HERRMANN
New Hope, Pennsylvania

ACKNOWLEDGMENTS

I would like to thank David Eller, Joanna Hill, and Stuart Shotwell for their support during the early days of this project, and through its initial publication in 1994. I am grateful to Mary Lou Bertucci, Deborah Forman, and Susan Picard of the Swedenborg Foundation for their continued contribution of energy, skill, and vision in bringing about this new edition. Unwilling to let Helen's inspired words fade from world consciousness, they have continued to explore ways in which Helen's work could be further refined and brought to more readers. In many ways, this book is the fruit of their vision and labor. My wife, Star, has been especially supportive throughout the many years that this project has been in progress, always reminding me, through her presence and example, that "love is the surest guide."

Sending off her manuscript to her publisher, Helen Keller wrote, "My joy will know no bounds if what I have written turns out to be worthy of the light-bringer to the souls of men who are lost in the horror of great darkness." In the same spirit, we pray that this edition of *Light in My Darkness* will be worthy of Helen Keller, the great and noble soul, who, while living in darkness, saw a great Light.

— RAY SILVERMAN
Huntingdon Valley, Pennsylvania

LIGHT IN MY DARKNESS

"SWEDENBORG"

A POEM BY HELEN KELLER

"Heaven unbarred to him her lofty gates . . ."
(Michelangelo, "On Dante")

O light-bringer of my blindness,
O spirit never far removed!
Ever when the hour of travail deepens,
Thou art near;
Set in my soul like jewels bright
Thy words of holy meaning,
Till Death with gentle hand shall lead me
    to the Presence I have loved—
My torch in darkness here,
My joy eternal there.

*That word "water" dropped into my mind
like the sun in a frozen winter world.*

AWAKENINGS

Unless one is born of water and the Spirit,
he cannot enter the kingdom of God. (John 3:5)

MY MENTAL AWAKENING

For nearly six years I had no concept whatsoever of nature or mind or death or God. I literally thought with my body. Without a single exception, my memories of that time are tactile.

I know I was impelled like an animal to seek food and warmth. I remember crying, but not the grief that caused the tears; I kicked, and because I recall it physically, I know I was angry. I imitated those about me when I made signs for things I wanted to eat, or helped to find eggs in my mother's farmyard. But there is not one spark of emotion or rational thought in these distinct yet corporeal memories.

I was like an unconscious clod of earth. There was nothing in me except the instinct to eat and drink and sleep. My days were a blank without past, present, or future, without hope or anticipation, without interest or joy.

It was not night—it was not day . . .
But vacancy absorbing space,
And fixedness—without a place;
There were no stars—no earth—no time—
No check—no change—no good—no crime.

(LORD BYRON, "THE PRISONER OF CHILLON")

Then suddenly, I knew not how or where or when, my brain felt the impact of another mind, and I awoke to language, to knowledge, to love, to the usual concepts of nature, good, and evil. I was actually lifted from nothingness to human life.

My teacher, Anne Mansfield Sullivan, had been with me nearly a month, and she had taught me the names of a number of objects. She put them into my hand, spelled their names on her fingers and helped me to form the letters; but I had not the faintest idea what I was doing. I do not know what I thought. I have only a tactile memory of my fingers going through those motions and changing from one position to another.

One day she handed me a cup and spelled the word. Then she poured some liquid into the cup and formed the letters w-a-t-e-r. She says I looked puzzled and persisted in confusing the two words, spelling cup for water and water for cup. Finally I became angry because Miss Sullivan kept repeating the words over and over again.

In despair, she led me out to the ivy-covered pumphouse and made me hold the cup under the spout while she pumped. With her other hand she spelled w-a-t-e-r emphatically. I stood still, my whole body's attention fixed on the motions of her fingers as the cool stream flowed over my hand. All at once there was a strange stir within me—a misty consciousness, a sense of

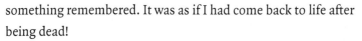

something remembered. It was as if I had come back to life after being dead!

I understood that what my teacher was doing with her fingers meant that the cold something that was rushing over my hand was water, and that it was possible for me to communicate with other people by these hand signs.

It was a wonderful day, never to be forgotten. Thoughts that ran forward and backward came to me quickly—thoughts that seemed to start in my brain and spread all over me. Now I see it was my mental awakening. I think it was an experience somewhat in the nature of a revelation. I showed immediately in many ways that a great change had taken place in me. I wanted to learn the name of every object I touched, and before night I had mastered thirty words. Nothingness was blotted out! I felt joyous, strong, equal to my limitations! Delicious sensations rippled through me, and sweet, strange things that were locked up in my heart began to sing.

When the sun of consciousness first shone upon me, behold a miracle! The stock of my young life that had perished, now steeped in the waters of knowledge, grew again, budded again, was sweet again with the blossoms of childhood. Down in the depths of my being I cried, "It is good to be alive!" I held out two trembling hands to life, and in vain would silence impose dumbness upon me henceforth.

That first revelation was worth all those years I had spent in dark, soundless imprisonment. That word "water" dropped into my mind like the sun in a frozen winter world.

The world to which I awoke was still mysterious; but there were hope and love and God in it, and nothing else mattered.

Is it not possible that our entrance into heaven may be like this experience of mine?

I INQUIRED ABOUT GOD

As a little child I naturally wanted to know who made everything in the world, and I was told that nature (they called it Mother Nature) had made earth and sky and water and all living creatures. This satisfied me for a time, and I was happy among the rose trees of my mother's garden, or on the bank of a river, or out in the daisy-covered fields, where my teacher told me Arabian Nights tales about seeds and flowers, birds and insects, and the fishes in the river. Like other children, I believed that every object I touched was alive and self-conscious, and I supposed we were all Mother Nature's children.

But as I grew older, I began to reason about the parts of nature I could touch. Obviously, I am using mature words and the ideas of later years to make intelligible the groping, half-formed, ever-shifting impressions of childhood. I noticed a difference between the way human beings did their work and the way the wonders of nature were wrought. I saw that puppies, flowers, stones, babies, and thunderstorms were not just put together as my mother mixed her hotcakes. There was an order and sequence of things in field and wood that puzzled me, and at the same time there was a confusion in the elements, which at times terrified me.

The wanton destruction of the beautiful and the ugly, the useful and the obnoxious, the righteous and the wicked by earthquake or flood or tornado I could not understand. How could such a blind mass of irresponsible forces create and keep things

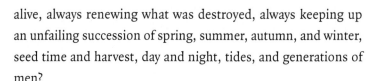

alive, always renewing what was destroyed, always keeping up an unfailing succession of spring, summer, autumn, and winter, seed time and harvest, day and night, tides, and generations of men?

Somehow I sensed that nature was no more concerned about me or those I loved than with a twig or a fly. This awoke in me something akin to resentment—"the fine innuendo by which the soul makes its enormous claim," and declares that it has a pre-rogative of control over the course of events and things.

Turning away from nature, I inquired about God, and again I was baffled. Friends tried to tell me that God was the creator, and that he was everywhere, that he knew all the needs, joys, and sorrows of every human life, and that nothing happened without his foreknowledge and providence. Some with a generous dispo-sition said God was merciful to all and caused the sun to shine on the just and the unjust alike. I was drawn irresistibly to such a glorious, lovable being, and I longed really to understand some-thing about him.

One day I asked my teacher why people could not see God, and I remember her answer: "This human body we live in is a veil that prevents us from seeing him." She illustrated this with a screen. She made me stand on one side of it, and she stood on the other side. We were quite hidden from each other. She could not see me, and I could not touch her; yet by little signs I knew she was there, only separated from me by that "veil" of Japanese paper.

Soon afterwards we visited Boston, and because I persisted in asking questions about God and Jesus—"Why did they kill him? Why does God make some people good and others bad? Why must we all die?"—Miss Sullivan took me to see Phillips Brooks, the gifted preacher and rector at Trinity Church. She felt that if anyone could answer my questions in a simple, beautiful way, he could. Her intuition did not fail her.

The great man understood the heart of a child. He took me on his knee, and told me in the simplest language how God loved me and every one of his children. He made God seem so real that I said, "O yes, I know him. I had just forgotten his name." Bishop Brooks told me the wonderful story of Jesus Christ, and my eyes filled with tears, and my heart beat with love for the gentle Nazarene who restored sight to the blind and speech to the mute, healed the sick, fed the hungry, and turned sorrow into joy. Indeed, I felt that the Lord's arms were about the whole world, as Mr. Brooks's arms were clasping me, in pitying tenderness. After that visit, my knowledge of the character and words of Christ grew day by day; I felt more and more his life deepening down into mine, and I found more and more to be glad of in the world.

But I could not form any clear idea of the relation between this Divine Love and the material world. I lost myself many times in shadows and uncertainties, wandering back and forth between the light that was so ineffably reassuring and the chaos and darkness of nature that seemed so real as not to be denied.

One day I was made radiantly happy and brought nearer to a sense of God when I "watched" in my mind's eye an exquisite butterfly, just out of its cocoon, drying its wings in the sun, and afterward felt it fluttering over a bunch of trailing arbutus. Someone told me how the ancient Egyptians had looked upon the butterfly as an emblem of immortality. I was delighted. It seemed to me as it should be, that such beautiful forms of life should have in them a lesson about things still more lovely. Nevertheless, the

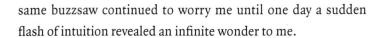

same buzzsaw continued to worry me until one day a sudden flash of intuition revealed an infinite wonder to me.

MY SPIRITUAL AWAKENING

I had been sitting quietly in the library for half an hour. I turned to my teacher and said, "Such a strange thing has happened! I have been far away all this time, and I haven't left the room."

"What do you mean, Helen?" she asked, surprised.

"Why," I cried, "I have been in Athens!"

Scarcely were the words out of my mouth when a bright, amazing realization seemed to catch my mind and set it ablaze. I perceived the realness of my soul and its sheer independence of all conditions of place and body. It was clear to me that it was because I was a spirit that I had so vividly "seen" and felt a place thousands of miles away. Space was nothing to spirit! In that new consciousness shone the presence of God, who is a spirit everywhere at once, the Creator dwelling in all the universe simultaneously.

The fact that my small soul could reach out over continents and seas to Greece, despite a blind, deaf, and stumbling body, sent another exulting emotion rushing over me. I had broken through my limitations and found in the sense of touch an eye. I could read the thoughts of wise men and women—thoughts that had for ages survived their mortal life—and could possess them as part of myself.

If this were true, how much more could God, the uncircumscribed spirit, cancel the harms of nature—accident, pain, destruction—and reach out to his children! Deafness and blindness, then, were of no real account. They were to be relegated to the outer circle of my life. Of course I did not sense any such process with my child-mind; but I did know that I, the real I, could leave the library and visit any place I wanted to, mentally, and I was happy. That was the little seed from which grew my interest in spiritual subjects.

JOHN HITZ

I was not at that time especially enthusiastic about Bible stories, except the story of the gentle Nazarene. The accounts of creation and the expulsion of Adam and Eve from the Garden of Eden for eating a particular fruit, the great flood, and all the wrath and vengeance of the Old Testament seemed to me very similar to the Greek and Roman myths I had read—and there were very few gods and goddesses I could admire.

I was disappointed not to find in the Bible that my good aunt held up to me as a divine book, a likeness of the God whose face shone so benign, beautiful, and radiant in my heart. She told me tales out of the book of Revelation, and still I felt a void I could not explain. What could I see in a war between God and dragons and horned beasts? How could I associate the eternal torture of those cast into the lake of fire with the God whom Christ declared to be love? Why, I wondered, should one particular City of God be described with pavements of gold and walls of precious stones when heaven must be full of everything else just as magnificent—mountains, fields, oceans, and the sweet, fruitful earth, restful to the feet? The touching story of Christ comforting the sorrowful, healing the sick, giving new light to the blind and speech to mute lips stirred me to the depths; but how could I worship three persons—the Father, the Son, and the Holy Ghost?

Was that not the sort of false worship so terribly punished in Old Testament days?

Such were the bewildered, dissatisfied thoughts on the Bible that possessed my mind when there came into my life one of the friends I would love most, John Hitz, who had for a long period held the position in Washington, D.C., of Consul-General for Switzerland. Afterward he was superintendent of the Volta Bureau in Washington, which Alexander Graham Bell founded with the Volta Prize money he received for inventing the telephone. This bureau was established for the purpose of collecting and distributing information about the deaf and publishing a magazine on their behalf called *The Volta Review.*

I first met Mr. Hitz in 1893, when I was about thirteen years old, and that was the beginning of an affectionate and beautiful friendship that I cherish among the dearest memories of my life. He was always interested in all I did—my studies, my girlish joys and dreams, my struggle through college, and my work for the blind. He had lost much of his hearing and was one of the few who fully appreciated my teacher, Miss Sullivan, and the special significance of her work not only to me but to all the world. His letters bore testimony to his affection for her and his understanding of what she was to me—a light in all dark places. He visited us often in Boston and Cambridge, and every time my teacher and I stopped over in Washington on our way to or from my southern home in Alabama, we had delightful visits with him.

After my teacher and I settled down in Wrentham, Massachusetts, he spent six weeks with us every summer until the year before he died. He loved to take me out walking early in the morning while the dew lay upon grass and tree, and the air was joyous with birdsongs. We wandered through still woods, fragrant meadows, past the picturesque stone walls of Wrentham, and always he brought me closer to beauty and the deep meaning of nature. As he talked, the great world shone for me in the glory of immortality. He stimulated in me the love of nature that is so precious a part of the music in my silence and the light in my darkness. It is sweet to recall the flowers and the laughing brooks and the shining, balmy moments of stillness in which we had joy together. Each day I beheld through his eyes a new and charming landscape, "wrapped in exquisite showers" of fancy and spiritual beauty. We would often pause that I might feel the swaying of the trees, the bending of the flowers, and the waving of the corn, and he would say, "The wind that puts all this life into nature is a marvelous symbol of the spirit of God."

On my fourteenth birthday, he presented me with a gold watch he had worn for more than thirty years, and I have never been separated from it since, except one time when it was sent to Switzerland for some parts that were worn out. Curiously enough, it was not made for the blind in the first place. It once belonged to a German ambassador who had it fixed so that he could keep important appointments exactly. He was obliged to call upon a high dignitary of the Kaiser, and it was not etiquette to look at the watch, nor was it etiquette to stay too long. So the Ambassador went to a jeweller and gave him instructions about making the watch so that he could slip his hand into his pocket and "feel" the time.

The watch has a crystal face and a gold hand on the back, which is connected with the minute hand and goes with it and stops with it. There are also gold points around the rim that indicate the hours. I wear it always against my heart, and it ticks for me as faithfully as my friend himself worked for me and loved me. He whose love it keeps ever before me has been gone many years, but I have the sweet consciousness that each tick is bringing me nearer and nearer to him. It is truly a treasure above price, linking time and eternity.

Mr. Hitz and I corresponded for many years. He learned the Braille system so that I could read myself his long and frequent letters. These letters are a record of spiritual kinship that it comforts me to read over when I long for the touch of his hand and the wise, inspiring words with which he encouraged me in my tasks. His first and last thought was how to lessen the obstacles I encountered. He quickly perceived my hunger for books I could read on subjects that particularly interested me, and how limited were the embossed books within my reach. For eight years he devoted a part of each day to copying whatever he thought would give me pleasure—stories, biographies of great men, and studies of nature.

Many friends have done wonderful things for me, but nothing like Mr. Hitz's untiring effort to share with me the inner sunshine and peace that filled his silent years. Each year I was drawn closer to him, and he wrote to me more constantly as the days passed. Then came a great sorrow—separation from the friend I loved best next to my teacher. I had been visiting my mother and was on my way back to Wrentham. As usual, I stopped in Washington, and Mr. Hitz came to the train to meet me. He was full of joy as he embraced me, saying how impatiently he had awaited my coming. Then, as he was leading me from the train, he had a sudden heart attack and passed away. Just before the end he took my hand, and I still feel his pressure when I think of that dark time. I could not have borne the loss of such an intimate and tender friend if I had thought he was indeed dead. But his noble philosophy and certainty of the life to come braced me with an unwavering faith that we should meet again in a world happier and more beautiful than anything of my dreaming. With me remains always the helpful memory of his rare personality.

He was a man of lofty character, a man of rich spiritual gifts. His heart was pure and warm, full of childlike faith in the best he saw in his fellow creatures, and he was always doing for other people something lovely and dear. In all his ways he kept the commandment, "Love thy neighbor as thyself" (Matthew 22:39). At eighty years of age, he had the heart of an evergreen, and his inexhaustible power of enjoyment lifted him far above the average of humanity. He remained young with the young. He was never old to me, and I was never deaf and blind to him. He spelled with difficulty on his fingers, and he was so hard of hearing I had often to repeat a sentence six times with my imperfect speech before he could understand me. But our love covered a multitude of difficulties, and our communication was always worth every effort it cost us.

HEAVEN AND HELL

In our many conversations, Mr. Hitz came to realize fully my hunger for literature on subjects that especially interested me. His own deafness had enabled him to see the distorted angle of my thoughts with regard to the world of the senses. He told me that if I would only try to put myself in the place of those with sight and hearing, and imagine their impressions of things, they could unite their senses with mine more and more, and thus wonderfully increase my enjoyment of the outer world. He showed me how I could find a key to their life and give them a chance to explore my own with understanding. He put into my hands a copy of Emanuel Swedenborg's *Heaven and Hell* in raised letters. He said he knew I would not understand much of it at first; but it was fine exercise for my mind, and it would satisfy me with a likeness of a God as lovable as the one in my heart.

When I began *Heaven and Hell*, I was as little aware of the new joy coming into my life as I had been years before when I stood on the piazza steps awaiting my teacher. Impelled only by the curiosity of a young girl who loves to read, I opened that big book, and lo, my fingers lighted upon a paragraph in the preface about a blind woman whose darkness was illumined with beautiful truths from Swedenborg's writings. She believed that they imparted a light to her mind that more than compensated for her loss of earthly light. She never doubted that there was a spiritual body within the material one with perfect senses and that after a few dark years, the eyes within her eyes would open to a world infinitely more wonderful, complete, and satisfying than this one.

My heart gave a joyous bound. Here was a faith that emphasized what I felt so keenly—the separateness between soul and body, between a realm I could picture as a whole and the chaos of fragmentary things and irrational contingencies which my limited physical senses met at every turn. I let myself go, as healthy, happy youth will, and tried to puzzle out the long words and the weighty thoughts of the Swedish sage. As I read *Heaven and Hell*, I felt God as close to me as when Bishop Brooks and I talked about Christ.

The words "Love" and "Wisdom" seemed to caress my fingers from paragraph to paragraph, and these two words released in me new forces to stimulate my somewhat indolent nature and urge me forward evermore. I came back to the book from time to time, picking up a line here and a line there, "precept upon precept," one glimpse, then another of the Divine Word hidden under the clouds of literal statement. As I realized the meaning of what I read, my soul seemed to expand and gain confidence amid the difficulties that beset me. The descriptions of the other world bore me far, far over measureless regions bathed in super-human beauty and strangeness. In that spiritual world where great lives and creative minds cast a splendor upon darkest circumstances, events and mighty combats sweep by endlessly, and the night is lit to eternal day by the smile of God.

I glowed through and through as I sat in that atmosphere of the soul and watched men and women of nobler mold pass in majestic procession. For the first time immortality put on intelligibility for me, and the earth wore new curves of loveliness and significance.

I was glad to discover that the City of God was not a stupid affair of glass streets and sapphire walls, but a systematic treasury of wise, helpful thoughts and noble influences. Gradually I came to see that I could use the Bible, which had so baffled me, as an instrument for digging out precious truths, just as I could use my hindered, halting body for the high behests of my spirit.

MY RELIGION

So I grew to womanhood, and as unaccountably as the Polish-born novelist Joseph Conrad found in English the language of his choice, I took more and more to the teachings of the New Church as my religion.

I cannot explain it any better than anyone else. I have many times tried to recall the feelings that led me to take Swedenborg's interpretation of Christianity rather than my father's Presbyterianism, but I can find no satisfactory answer. It was with me as it was with Conrad, when an irresistible impulse urged him to go to sea. Like him, I took a "standing jump" out of my associations and traditions—and the rest is what I have grown to be.

I do not know whether I adopted the faith or the faith adopted me. I can only say that the heart of the young girl sitting with a big book of raised letters on her lap in the sublime sunshine was thrilled by a radiant presence and inexpressibly endearing voice. There, with another of Swedenborg's books, *Divine Love and Wisdom*, spiritually bright, I read words that gave me eyes and gathered thoughts that quickened my ear. As the air is made luminous by the sun, so the Word ineffable makes bright all darkness.

I was not "religious" in the sense of practicing ritual, but happy, because I saw God altogether lovely, after the shadows cast upon his image by the harsh creeds of warring sects and religions. The Word of God, freed from the blots and stains of barbarous creeds, has been at once the joy and good of my life. It is wonderfully linked with my growing appreciation of my teacher's work and my own responsibilities of service, hours of struggle and solitude, hours of deepest joy, harsh truths faced squarely, and high dreams held dearer than the baits of ease and complaisance.

Those truths have been to my faculties what light, color, and music are to the eye and ear. They have opened the gate of the Garden of Heaven for me and showed me fair flowering paths where I love to walk. What precious herbs of healing grow there! What sweet smells of celestial flowers greet me! What thresholds of quiet I pass over, leaving behind me all the harsh, loud futilities of earth-life. There the Lamb of God walks in beauty through the grass. In the Garden of the Lord sparkle countless rills and fountains. There the dews from Hermon fall upon my head. The trees, laden with golden fruit, murmur wisdom with their leaves, and the birds no longer sing wordless notes, but immortal truths. There, blessed figures arrayed in light pass me and smile companionship with me; their beautiful hands guide me in paths of peace, and they whisper patience to me while I wait for my release into greater service and a more satisfying self-expression.

In giving me the golden key to the hidden treasures of the Bible, Swedenborg's books have lifted my wistful longing for a fuller sense-life into a vivid consciousness of the complete being within me. Each day comes to me with both hands full of possibilities, and in its brief course I discern all the verities and realities of my existence, the bliss of growth, the glory of action, the spirit of beauty.

Yes, the teachings of Emanuel Swedenborg have been my light and a staff in my hand, and by his vision splendid I am attended on my way.

SWEDENBORG'S SEARCH

You will seek me and find me, when you search
for me with all your heart. (Jeremiah 29:13)

THE AGE OF REASON

Hans Christian Anderson, the Danish writer, describes in one of his beautiful tales a garden where giant trees grew out of pots that were too small for them. Their roots were cruelly cramped; yet they lifted themselves up bravely into the sunlight, flung abroad their glorious branches, showered their wealth of blossoms, and refreshed weary mortals with their golden fruit. Into their hospitable arms came all singing birds, and ever in their hearts was a song of renewal and joy. At last they burst the hard, cold shackles that confined them and spread out their mighty roots in the sweetness of liberty.

To my mind that strange garden symbolizes the eighteenth century out of which grew the titan genius of Emanuel Swedenborg. Some have called that century the Age of Reason or the Enlightenment; others have characterized it as the coldest, most depressing time in human history. It is true, progress was wonderful everywhere. There were great philosophers, statesmen, and fearless investigators in science. Governments were better organized, the feudal system was held in check, and the public highways rendered more safe than they ever had been. The fiery passions of medievalism were curbed by a severe decorum and the iron scepter of reason.

But at that period, as in the Middle Ages before it, there was a sinister, oppressive atmosphere of sadness and sullen resignation. Able scholars like the French historian H. A. Taine have noted how a bitter theology treated man as a despised child of sin and gave the world over to the wrath of God. Even the gentle angel Charity, whom the saints of old had welcomed, was driven from man's side; faith alone was exalted, and not faith either, but a self-centered assumption that belief alone was necessary to salvation. All useful work seemed a vanity, all physical misfortunes were looked upon as punishments, and the darkest of all nights, ignorance and insensibility, lay upon the heart-starved world.

Such was the age out of whose harsh environment the genius of Swedenborg grew and whose fettering dogmas he was destined to shatter, as the giant trees in the tale burst their bonds. When such a thinker is "let loose upon the world," it is of special interest to recall some of the historic events and personalities centered round his own time.

Swedenborg was born not long after the death of John Amos Comenius, the heroic Czech educator and Moravian leader who dealt the first effectual blow at the giant of scholasticism that had for so long a time stalked through the Old World. The year of Swedenborg's birth, 1688, was the year of the fateful though bloodless revolution in England. He lived during the most magnificent part of the reign of King Louis XIV of France, and the memory of the bitter siege of La Rochelle was still raw in the minds of French Protestants. He witnessed the astonishing expeditions of Charles XII of Sweden. He was a contemporary of Carolus Linnaeus, the Swedish botanist. During Swedenborg's last years, Jean Jacques Rousseau in France spread his great doctrine of education according to nature, and Denis Diderot developed his philosophy of the senses and declared to the world that the blind could be taught. Perhaps no man was ever so precariously situated between traditions of a crumbling civilization and the sudden onrush of a new age toward which his forward-looking mind yearned.

The more I consider Swedenborg's position, the less I can see how we are to account for him, except as a miracle, so little did he have in common with his church or the standards of his century. I have not been able to discover anything about the circumstances of his birth and early training that seems to explain the most independent movement ever started in the history of religious thought. Thousands of others have been born of devout parents and admirably educated just as he was, and they have not contributed a new thought or increased the happiness of mankind. But then, is not it ever thus with genius—an angel entertained by us unawares?

THE DANGER OF SEEKING VISIONS

Swedenborg's home was Stockholm, Sweden. His parents were earnest people. His father, Jesper Swedenborg, was a Lutheran bishop, a professor of theology, a chaplain at the royal court, and a man of spiritual thought. Martin Luther, the great Protestant reformer, reportedly saw spirits and heard their voices, and many of his followers observed severe fasts and vigils so that they, too, might have glimpses of another world. It is said that the boy Emanuel had some such experiences. In later life he wrote to a friend: "From my fourth to my tenth year I was constantly engaged in thought upon God, salvation, and the spiritual experiences of men; and several times I revealed things at which my father and mother wondered, saying that angels must be speaking through me." Though his father may have been sympathetic, his mother interposed with decision and told her husband that Emanuel "must stop all such celestial excursions." Emanuel Swedenborg did not see a light or hear a sound from the spiritual world from that time until he was fifty-six years old. (Tafel 1877, II: 279)

From all his religious writings, it is clear that Swedenborg had no use for that kind of experience for children or for unprepared men and women. Of all people, he was in a position to realize the danger of seeking visions, and he frequently warns his readers against this most harmful practice.

His childhood was as beautiful a beginning as could be desired for a marvelous life. He and his father were constant companions. They climbed the hills around Stockholm and explored the fjords, collecting mosses, flowers, and brightly colored stones. When they returned, the child wrote long reports of their outdoor experiences. For he was a scholar from childhood, and his mind always outran the limits of his body. But, unlike many precocious young people, he grew strong and healthy, and his noble, manly bearing was much commented upon.

HIS MISSION WAS TO KNOW

Swedenborg received the best education the age and his country afforded. He attended the University of Uppsala, and it is said that his earliest productions display much poetical talent. But he devoted himself chiefly to mathematics and mechanics. He surprised his instructors by simplifying some most difficult processes in calculus, and often they could hardly follow his swift mind as it threaded the mazes of learning. They regarded him with awe, and the other students spoke of him in low tones.

It seems he was an unconscious mirror of the straitlaced tenets and solemn ways amid which he was brought up. His face was described as stern, though not forbidding. He was rather statuesque, but very handsome, with a commanding personality. He was never known to unbend to the gaieties and sports of youth; he could not even in later life profess his love to the shy young girl who inspired the only passion he ever knew. He went to her father, the distinguished inventor Christopher Polhem, instead of to her, and would have proved his love as if by means of charts and diagrams. The father was willing and gave the young man a warrant for the girl returnable in three years, but she was so frightened that her brother finally persuaded Swedenborg to give her up. But his love for her he never surrendered.

He was graduated from the University of Uppsala with honors, receiving the degree of Doctor of Philosophy in 1709, when he was twenty-one years of age. Afterward he traveled in foreign countries, not for pleasure but to learn. Swedenborg's close friend, Carl Robsahm, says in his Memoirs that in addition to the learned languages, he well understood French, English, Dutch, German, and Italian, for he had journeyed several times in these countries.

Swedenborg's father wished him to enter the diplomatic service, but he chose instead the paths of science. He was given letters of introduction to the rulers of Europe, but he calmly ignored them and sought out the most distinguished scholars of his day. Sometimes he would call unannounced—and ask for an interview. However, there was something about him that inspired their respect, and they seldom declined his request. His one desire, his mission, was to know, and he levied tribute upon everyone who had new ideas or methods or processes to impart.

DISCOVERING THE SECRETS OF NATURE

His profound learning brought him into close association with Christopher Polhem, who enjoyed the entire confidence of Charles XII of Sweden. In this way, Swedenborg was introduced to the king, who in 1716 appointed him assayer in the Swedish College of Mines, that is, an official who gives advice as to the best methods of working mines and smelting ores. With this appointment, Swedenborg entered upon a period of amazingly prodigious and diversified activity. Not only did he discharge the duties of his office faithfully and with wisdom, but he also pursued his studies in every department of science. As an independent thinker, he followed the urge of a powerful and original genius to discover, if possible, the deepest secrets of nature. He was as familiar with forge and quarry, workshop and shipyard, as he was with the stars and songs of birds in the morning. The flowers he found blooming in obscure nooks spoke to him secrets as marvelous as those of the majestic mountains he trod. His was a rare blending of the practical and the beautiful, mathematics and poetry, invention and literary power.

In 1718 Swedenborg turned his mechanical skill to account with Sweden's siege of Fredrikshald when he constructed machines by which to transport several large vessels a distance of fourteen miles overland, across hills and valleys. He worked on plans for a mechanical carriage—very complicated internally—for a flying carriage, and for a vessel to travel under the sea, thus foreshadowing the automobile, the airplane, and the submarine. He worked on plans for new machines for condensing and exhausting air by means of water. He tried to produce a universal musical instrument on which one quite unacquainted with music might execute all kinds of airs that were marked on paper with notes, and he contrived a way of ascertaining the desires and affections of people by analytical study. He devised an air gun capable of discharging a thousand bullets a minute! He had plans for drawbridges and various other mechanical devices. In him was prefigured the wonderful system of interrelated sciences and arts to which we owe the extraordinary progress of modern times. He showed how the decimal system could be of practical use. He caught marvelous glimpses of knowledge and theories that would be developed a century and a half later—paleontology, biology, meteorology; he outlined an atomic theory and the nebular hypothesis years in advance of the French astronomer and mathematician P. S. Laplace.

A COLOSSAL TREASURE OF KNOWLEDGE

Swedenborg was not blind to the great wealth and influence that these manifold attainments and abilities would bring within his reach. But he refused the cup of happiness lifted to his lips. The sorrows and oppression of humanity lay heavy upon his heart.

Humbled, shamed in his soul, he beheld the cruelties of a Christian theology that rained damnation upon myriads of human beings. Jonathan Edwards in the Great Awakening in New England at that time preached hellfire and fear; the countless babies that died unbaptized were consigned to everlasting torment. We moderns cannot conceive how the ingenuity of evil was exerted to turn God's Word into a curse. Heaven was monstrous, hell unspeakable, and life one long misery. Swedenborg said to himself, "What is the use of all the knowledge I have gained when such a hideous shadow lies vast across the world?" He turned away from the splendors of fame and spent twenty-nine years—one third of his life—in comparative poverty, comforting the hurt souls of his fellow men with a humane, reasonable doctrine of faith and life.

Besides all his other labors, he wrote during every spare hour he could crowd in, and he produced altogether some sixty books and pamphlets before the beginning of his inquiries in the field of religion. Among the great works of this period were *The First Principles of Natural Things*, *The Brain*, *The Economy of the Animal Kingdom*, and *Rational Psychology*.

Speaking of those scientific productions, the American philosopher Ralph Waldo Emerson observed:

> It seems that he anticipated much of the science of the nineteenth century. . . . His writings would be a sufficient library to a lonely and athletic student; and *The Economy of the Animal Kingdom* is one of those books which, by the sustained dignity of its thinking, is an honor to the human race. *The Animal Kingdom* is a book of wonderful merits. It was written with the highest

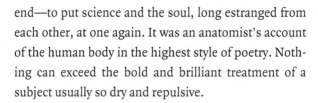

end—to put science and the soul, long estranged from each other, at one again. It was an anatomist's account of the human body in the highest style of poetry. Nothing can exceed the bold and brilliant treatment of a subject usually so dry and repulsive.

Editor and writer Elbert Hubbard remarked that Charles Darwin seemed to have read *The First Principles of Natural Things* with the most minute care. At any rate, Swedenborg divined something of evolution when he saw in a tiny lichen on a rock the beginning of a forest. He also waived the literal account of creation in the Bible as a contradiction of scientific facts. It should be added that he never in any of his religious writings changed his attitude toward Genesis. In fact, he ridiculed and tore down the time-honored shrine of Biblical literalism, but at the same time discovered in Scripture what he called a most ancient style of narrative that had nothing at all to do with the physical creation, but was a long-forgotten parable of the human soul.

Besides mathematics, mechanics, and mining, Swedenborg shows in his works an intimate knowledge of chemistry, anatomy, and geology, and a fondness for music. His philosophical subjects were almost equally varied and extensive. Yet he always had time "to render himself in all things useful to society." For many years he was a member of the Swedish Parliament, and on account of his distinguished services to his country he was highly honored. Many distinctions were conferred upon him as time passed. In 1724 the Consistory of the University of Uppsala invited him to accept a position as professor of pure mathematics, but he declined. He was admitted as a member of several institutions of learning in St. Petersburg, Uppsala, and Stockholm. His portrait is in the hall of the Royal Academy of Sciences at Stockholm, as one of its distinguished members, hanging near that of Linnaeus, whose system of classifying plants and animals revolutionized the study of botany.

Swedenborg's life, in a word, seems to have been nothing but work, work, always work. He became financially independent, but this only spurred him on to accomplish more. All persons, regardless of their station in life, bore testimony to his noble character and selfless devotion. As he grew older, his kind ways endeared him to all his intimate friends, and the sternness that characterized his young manhood melted away.

But real companionship he never knew. He had climbed too high on the ladder of thought even for his fellow-scientists to converse with him on some of the subjects with which he was familiar. They did not attempt to read his works, but preferred to recommend them. No one seemed able or willing to follow his giant strides into the upper realm of speculation. He was an eye among the blind, an ear among the deaf, a voice crying in the wilderness with a language they could not understand.

I cannot help thinking he was lonely with more than earthly loneliness, and the world seemed strange to him because he had already outgrown it. Perhaps no one had ever endured such a pressure of soul against the prison bars of flesh as he did, and there was no reassuring nearness of equal intelligence to lighten his burden. He had given his life to learn, and what could he do with his colossal treasure of knowledge? He was naturally glad when more light and more opportunity was let into his difficult days; but I question whether he ever felt quite at home upon earth after his "illumination."

SWEDENBORG'S ILLUMINATION

In about the year 1744 a great change came upon Swedenborg. This keen observer of natural facts and analyzer of things of the mind was given from on high powers of observation of things spiritual; the senses of his spirit were quickened to recognize realities in the spiritual world. His friend, Carl Robsahm, records a conversation in which he asked Swedenborg where and how it was granted him to see and to hear what takes place in the world of spirits, in heaven, and in hell. The answer was that in the night one had come to him and said:

> that He was the Lord God, the Creator of the world, and the Redeemer, and that He had chosen me to explain to men the spiritual sense of the Scripture, and that He Himself would explain to me what I should write on this subject; that same night also were opened to me, so that I became thoroughly convinced of their reality, the world of spirits, heaven, and hell, and I recognized there many acquaintances of every condition in life. From that day I gave up the study of all worldly science, and labored in spiritual things, according as the Lord had commanded me to write. Afterwards the Lord opened, daily very often, my bodily (*lekamlig*) eyes so that in the middle of the day I could see into the other world, and in a state of perfect wakefulness converse with angels and spirits. (Tafel 1875, I: 36)

In September of 1766, Swedenborg wrote to Frederick C. Oetinger, a Lutheran church official in Württemberg:

> I can solemnly bear witness that the Lord Himself has appeared to me, and that He has sent me to do that

which I am doing now, and that for this purpose He
has opened the interiors of my mind, which are those
of my spirit, so that I may see those things which are in
the spiritual world and hear those who are there, and
which privilege I have had now for twenty-two years.
(Tafel 1877, II: 249)

This privileged communication continued to the date of his
death on March 29, 1772, while he was temporarily residing in
London.

Swedenborg looked upon his highest concepts as a revelation
from the infinite mind of God. In fact, from his own words it is
clear he did not regard his conscious presence in the spiritual
world as an end in itself. Rather, it was a means of developing
the other half of his understanding, which as a rule is dormant in
us, and seeing more comprehensively different kinds of concepts
of good and evil, of spirit and matter, and translating the Bible
into living principles instead of mere words and phrases. He did
not say he was the only person who had had that kind of vision.
Far from it. What he did say was that he lived twenty-nine years
in full consciousness of the real world where all men live at the
same time they inhabit the earth.

SWEDENBORG'S NEW MISSION

Swedenborg believed that it was his mission to search out and
interpret the "spiritual sense" or sacred symbolism of Scripture,
and that his experiences in the other world were to help him to
understand truly the Word of God and convey the most wonderful and beneficent truths to mankind. Therefore, Swedenborg
devoted himself with all his former energy and courage to the

investigation of the facts and laws of the soul realm. He took up the study of Hebrew, so that he might read the Old Testament in the original language and gain a firsthand knowledge of the religious forms and parables and mysteries of ancient times.

It is evident that for many years he had endeavored to grasp the meaning of countless obscure passages in the Bible and had constantly felt baffled. Many things had troubled him: tradition and the almost unconquerable habit of sectarian interpretation, the coldness of an age that left out of Christianity its very heart of love, the witchcraft of a church literature ably and brilliantly advocating tenets that were never dreamed of by any prophet or apostle, and finally the obsessing illusions of the senses. But at last the light broke upon his mind—the truth made him free— and he gave all his magnificent powers to the release of the world.

In 1747, Swedenborg asked and obtained leave of Frederick I, the King of Sweden, to retire from the office of assessor, so that he might not be disturbed in his new work. A higher degree of rank was offered him, but he refused, fearing that it might inspire him with pride. Thus, he withdrew quietly from the splendors of a notable society and the honors with which he had been crowned to the seclusion of his little library, where he produced numerous books, the sole object of which was to make Christianity a living reality upon earth.

Whatever may be the opinions of those who read Swedenborg's religious books, they cannot but be impressed by his unique personality. He did everything gently and deliberately. There was nothing of excitement or elation about him. The farther he traveled in the spiritual realm, the more humble and composed he became. He refused to appeal to the weakness or credulity of the ignorant. He did not attempt to make any proselytes; nor did he wish to have his name associated with a New Church, which he said the Lord was about to establish in the world. He felt that his message was for posterity rather than for his generation; and as his works—the result of long, hard years of labor—left the press in large Latin folios, he distributed them at his own expense among the universities and the clergy of Europe. He did not even put his name to many of his works: "Servant of the Lord Jesus Christ" was his pen name.

Swedenborg, the man, was as lofty and noble as his work. He was one of those intellectual giants who come into the world no more than once a century and astonish it with the vastness of their learning and their multitudinous activity.

The poet Walt Whitman says that "we convince by our presences," and that is powerfully true of the Swedish seer as he worked at his colossal task. He fully realized the incredulity and hostility with which many of his statements would be viewed, and he could have rendered them more attractive by omitting or softening down unpleasant truths in a charming and entertaining manner. Yet he never flinched or turned aside from his high trust. When he passed out of the body that had become so painfully inadequate to his soaring mind, a degree of obloquy fell upon his illustrious name; and for a time one of the noblest champions true Christianity has ever known was nearly forgotten. The only reward he ever knew in his growing isolation upon earth was the consciousness that he was giving his full measure of devotion to the welfare and happiness of all people.

There are some lines by John Drinkwater in his play *Lincoln* that always bring Swedenborg vividly before me:

One of the noblest champions
true Christianity has ever known.

Lonely is the man who understands.
Lonely is vision that leads a man away
From the pasture-lands,
From the furrows of corn and the brown loads of hay
To the mountain-side,
To the high places where contemplation brings
All his adventurings
Among the sowers and the tillers in the wide
Valleys to one fused experience,
That shall control
The course of his soul,
And give his hand
Courage and continence.

With matchless constancy the seer possessed his soul in loneliness and vision. He was a man whose life was so unique, so wonderful, that anyone who studies it must become as humble as a little child.

SWEDENBORG'S ACCOMPLISHMENTS

Open my eyes that I may behold wondrous
things out of thy law. (Psalm 119:18)

A COLOSSAL SOUL

Do I hear someone say, "But is not deaf and blind Helen Keller liable to be imposed upon by those whose opinions or dogmas or political ideals are confined to a small minority?" Before considering Swedenborg's claims, which have astonished the world ever since they were made, I should like to lay before the reader the opinions of well-known writers who were conversant with his works but who have had no affiliations with the church that treasures his religious teachings.

It will be remembered that Emerson chose Swedenborg as one of his *Representative Men.* He says:

> This man, who appeared to his contemporaries a visionary and elixir of moonbeams, no doubt led the most real life of any man then in the world. . . . A colossal soul, he lies vast abroad on his times, uncomprehended by them, and requires a long focal distance to be seen.

It should be noted in passing that Emerson had no eye for Swedenborg's hell or mind for his Bible symbolism.

Essayist and historian Thomas Carlyle was a canny Scot not likely to be led astray. This is his estimate of Swedenborg:

> A man of great and indisputable cultivation, strong, mathematical intellect, and the most pious, seraphic turn of mind; a man beautiful, lovable, and tragical to me. . . . More truths are confessed in his writings than in those of any other man. . . . One of the loftiest minds in the realm of mind. . . . One of the spiritual suns that will shine brighter as the years go on.

Elbert Hubbard's comparison between Swedenborg and Shakespeare is of special interest, as he approaches the subject from an entirely different angle:

> They are Titans both. In the presence of such giants, small men seem to wither and blow away. Swedenborg was cast in a heroic mold, and no man since history began ever compassed in himself so much physical science, and, with it all on his back, made such daring voyages into the clouds. The men who soar highest and know most about another world usually know little about this. No man of his time was so competent a scientist as Swedenborg, and no man before or since has mapped so minutely the Heavenly Kingdom.

Philosopher Henry James, Sr., said, "Emanuel Swedenborg had the sanest and most far-reaching intellect this age has known." American poet Edwin Markham said that "Swedenborg's writings are today the prime influence beating down the wall of irrationality, making way for a faith that appeals at once to reason and to the heart." And Honoré de Balzac, the great French author, writes, "Swedenborg undoubtedly epitomizes all the religions—or rather the one religion—of humanity."

There are others who bear interesting witness to the impression left upon them by Swedenborg's teachings. Among them was Elizabeth Barrett Browning, whose beauty of soul and exquisite poetry excited such admiration everywhere. "To my mind," she says, "the only light that has been cast on the other life is found in Swedenborg's philosophy. It explains much that was incomprehensible."

Poet and critic Samuel Taylor Coleridge pays this tribute to one who has been hastily called by some a madman:

> I can venture to assert, as a moralist, Swedenborg is above all praise; and that, as a naturalist, psychologist, and theologian, he has strong and varied claims on the gratitude and admiration of the professional and philosophical faculties. . . . Thrice happy should we be if the learned teachers of today were gifted with a like madness!

Such estimates by these distinguished men and women are helpful in forming some idea of the personality and commanding genius Swedenborg possessed. Any defect there may be in my own judgment of him is evidently not due to my physical limitations. Measured by those who are scholars themselves, and by others who are esteemed for spiritual gifts, he is proclaimed to have had an amazingly well-trained intellect—trained, as Emerson observes, "to work with astronomic precision."

If he had been an illiterate man, no matter how wonderful his experience and how authentic his claims, he could not long have stood his ground before the pitiless battery of competent inquiry. But here is a scholar far ahead of his time, mastering the arts and sciences, writing able and voluminous works on every wonder of nature from the tiny lichen on the rocks to the most complex structure of the brain, always preserving a splendid balance on dizzy heights of learning where he must climb alone; and then with the same audacity, calmness, and composure, feeling his perilous way over the depths and abysses of the spirit-world and revealing with fearless authority the delicate yet unbreakable links between mind and matter, eternity and time, God and man.

Three of my dear friends have had something to say of Swedenborg, and they would not have said it of a lunatic or an intolerant fanatic. I knew longest Edward Everett Hale, the Unitarian clergyman, and I always marveled at his freshness of interest in all things and the variety of subjects upon which he deeply pondered. It was he who passed this judgment: "Swedenborgianism has done the liberating work of the last century. The wave Swedenborg started lasts to this day. The statements of his religious works have revolutionized theology."

Like all who loved Bishop Phillips Brooks, I realize what weight and significance his public utterances carry with them. His opinion on this subject is surely deserving of consideration:

> I have the profoundest honor for the character and work of Emanuel Swedenborg. . . . I have from time to time gained much from his writings. It is impossible to say a little on so great a theme. Yes, in a true sense, we are all New Churchmen, with new light, new hopes, and new communion with God in Christ.

And John Greenleaf Whittier, the dear mystic poet, said,

> There is one grand and beautiful idea underlying all
> his revelations about the future life. . . . His revelations
> look through all external and outward manifestations
> to inward realities; which regard all objects in the world
> of sense only as the types and symbols of the world of
> spirit; literally unmasking the universe and laying bare
> the profoundest mysteries of life.

A SPIRITUAL PIONEER

Another way to appreciate Swedenborg, the man, is to compare
him with other great world leaders. In science, literature, and
philosophy there are those who stand like heralds on mountain-
tops proclaiming a new day, of which they catch the first rays.
There are patriots who deliver their country from a cruel yoke or
lead the people to a truer freedom. There are those who search
the treasures of earth and discover new stores of light and heat;
there are those who reveal countless stars and distant planets,
and still others who sail many seas and find not a Northwest Passage but an America. Finally, in religion there are leaders who
teach millions by example or precept, who destroy idolatry or
who awaken the temple or church from superstitions and hypocrisy; and again others, like John Wesley, the father of Methodism,
who pour love into the coldness of an unspiritual age.

Michelangelo saw an angel in the stone and "carved it with
a sharp incision until he caught the vision." But Swedenborg's
inner eyes were opened to behold living angels, and out of the literal truths of the Bible, which are its stones, he carved heavenly
messages of love and help from God to his children.

From our childhood we have been familiar with the characters of Napoleon, Wellington, Washington, and Grant, and the fearful battles they took part in. But it was Swedenborg's lot to witness war between the forces of good and evil in the spiritual world. Armed with the weapons of heaven (the new doctrines of the Word) and the sword of earth (the truths of nature), he is the greatest champion of genuine Christianity in twenty centuries. Alexander II of Russia set the serfs free, and Lincoln abolished slavery in the United States. Over a temple of religion in the spiritual world Swedenborg saw written, "Now it is permitted to enter intellectually into the mysteries of faith," and he gave mankind a spiritual philosophy that liberated their minds and overthrew the power of ecclesiastical despotism. What others did in science and politics, Swedenborg did in religion. With massive arguments and thundering anathemas, he sent a continent's literature of pessimism, condemnation, and insincerity crashing down into the abyss.

Columbus's undaunted faith was realized in the discovery for Europe of a new continent, and Vasco de Balboa "stood on a peak in Darien" with the Pacific Ocean immense upon his vision. Now we have before us an explorer who traveled through the "undiscovered country," heard its language with his ears, conversed with its inhabitants, and described to our world, "from things heard and seen," its life, climate, and civilization.

Finally, in forming an idea of Swedenborg's place in the life thought of the world, we may recall the religious teachers of humanity: Buddha lived his gentle life, which shone as an example before the peoples of the Orient; Confucius taught by precept; and Muhammed carried his message of one God with fire and sword through lands given over to idolatry. Swedenborg strove to impart a sane, clear-eyed faith—rational truths that alone can protect religion from ignorance, brute force, and the cunning of those who would use it as a means of oppression. Those other leaders, earnest and sincere as they were, did not possess the science, the perception of human motives, and the militant truths that alone can prevent society from forging fetters for the minds and bodies of men.

Luther protested against the superstitious practices of the medieval church, and the Reformation began. Wesley broke down the formality of the Church of England, and the enthusiastic service of his followers to humanity is now worldwide. But many of the fundamental teachings remain, and a noble exponent of the Roman Catholic faith, Cardinal John Henry Newman, whose *Apologia* I read attentively years ago, laid bare great inconsistencies that ought to be faced squarely by all Protestants. Swedenborg brought to all sects in Christendom an abundance of new truths; he was the Herald of a new dispensation.

THE LORD'S SECOND COMING

Whatever opinion may be formed of the nature or the values of Swedenborg's claims, it is obvious that his experience is a unique one. No other man, highly trained in all the sciences of his time, has ever asserted that he was in constant communication with another world for more than a quarter of a century, while possessing all his faculties intact. Partial, occasional, even frequent and habitual glimpses of the spirit realm are recorded in every age and everywhere. Moses had visions of God and new life for his people. Through him the sacred symbolism of the Jewish

He was the Herald of a new dispensation.

dispensation was given, and he understood the importance of leading the Israelites out of slavery to a new civilization; but he did not sense the divine message couched in the Word for the human race. The Hebrew prophets, also, had visions and heard voices; but Isaiah, Jeremiah, and Daniel were evidently unaware of the higher truths they were conveying to all peoples symbolically. Most of them saw only the narrower historical meaning of the message.

The apostle Paul comprehended many truths of the Hebrew Scripture spiritually, and his epistles are more illuminating than all those of the other apostles put together. He was caught up into the third heaven but could not tell what he saw. Indeed, he said he did not know whether he was in the body or out of it. These instances were, so to speak, reports of local events in a strange country, while Swedenborg was consciously admitted to that strange country and prepared by long observation to make known the life and laws of heaven, the world of spirits, and hell.

The apostle of love, John, beheld in vision the future state of the Christian world and the glory of a new humanity. What John saw in symbol, Swedenborg saw in reality. It was Swedenborg's task to bear witness to the fulfillment of those prophetic pictures and to explain every scene, so that John's Revelation is no longer a sealed book. It lies open, its seals broken and its meaning shining with the splendor of Christ's second coming.

"An incredible claim!" I hear someone exclaim. Yet it seems to me less incredible than the claim that a native of Stratford-on-Avon, with scarcely any classical education and no advantages whatsoever, should have produced thirty-eight immortal plays. What Emanuel Swedenborg with his "vast, indisputable cultivation" did claim is that he was divinely called and prepared to interpret the stories, symbols, and other mysteries of the Bible. His special mission was to disclose the influences of another world that we often "feel" so vividly, and to gladden the deserts of life with new ideas of will, wisdom, power, and joy. That, he declared, heralded the second coming of the Lord, a coming to man in a doctrine of right living and true thinking. If this seems incredible, it should be remembered that that is what most people say of anything uncommon.

We might remember that in 1880 certain men knew that flying-machines could be equipped and rendered safe; but few would listen to them because such a thing had never been done. So flying came slowly, as the achievement of a small, faithful minority laboring in an atmosphere of ridicule.

There are other funds of knowledge building up. We know, for instance, that it is possible to plan the economic systems in the world so that we could all be much richer and freer and happier in producing comforts and pleasures than we are today. We know with at least an equal certainty that we can reorganize the whole educational system so that the bulk of humanity will grow up more happily prepared for creative service. We know that the international troubles of our time, the hostilities between peoples, the menace of war, are largely due to mental concepts that can be changed only by suggestion, persistence, training, and sheer devotion to humanity. Nations have become so dependent one upon another for the support of life that war is more than ever madness. Yet so-called educated people are incredulous of social, political, and spiritual developments they may live to see and share. The small group of believers who know must struggle

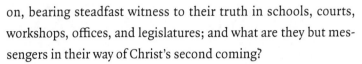

on, bearing steadfast witness to their truth in schools, courts, workshops, offices, and legislatures; and what are they but messengers in their way of Christ's second coming?

"But how can I accept such an audacious and extraordinary claim, contrary to everything I have observed?" someone again demands. It is true that when we read the works of other authors we have accepted rules and canons of criticism to guide us; but in the case of Swedenborg, we have almost none. From the very nature of such a case, we can know little or nothing about the psychological states through which he passed, except what he himself reports. His own testimony must convince us, if anything can.

That is nothing new to my experience. Daily I place implicit faith in my friends with their eyes and ears, and they tell me how often their senses deceive and lead them astray. Yet out of their evidence, I gather countless precious truths with which I build my world, and my soul is enabled to picture the beauty of the sky and listen to the songs of birds. All about me may be silence and darkness, yet within me, in the spirit, is music and brightness; and color flashes through all my thoughts. So out of Swedenborg's evidence from beyond earth's frontier, I construct a world that shall measure up to the high claims of my spirit when I quit this wonderful but imprisoning house of clay.

All things upon earth represent and image
forth all the realities of another world.

INTO THE HOLY OF HOLIES
When the Spirit of truth comes, he will
guide you into all the truth. (John 16:13)

THE DANGER OF LITERALISM

The Bible is the record of humanity's effort to find God and learn
how to live in harmony with divine law. Theologians have always
endeavored to grip in permanent form people's momentary
impressions of God and the fleeting, changing aspects of the
world. From this process have arisen many of the contradictions
in the literal sense of the Bible, and misunderstandings of God's
nature and God's purpose. The Bible tells of humanity's halting
beginning and gradual development, and of its culminating perfection in the Christ-gospel.

I conceive of this wonderful book as a spiritual *Iliad* covering
many thousands of years, touching many nations—a splendid,
variegated story, crossed at certain points by uninspired individual imaginings, dark periods of materialism, and illuminated
periods when the face of God shone upon the world, and there

was light on field and sky and water and in the minds of men and women. Out of the chaos of human experience, an individual is now and then lifted to the peak of spiritual consciousness. As humanity develops and our intelligence slowly unfolds, these individual peaks are more frequently seen; but they are never precisely alike. Each one is a light-bringer; but the light is so infinitely varied by the medium through which it is transmitted that it is sometimes difficult to perceive its divine source.

Just as all things upon earth represent and image forth all the realities of another world, so the Bible is one mighty representative of the whole spiritual life of humanity. Through its pages the characters come and pass before us—the lawgivers, the kings, the prophets. Like a mountain stream, the generations pass in endless procession, now praying, now weeping, now filling the cities with the voice of rejoicing, now walking in the evil imaginings of their hearts and making unto themselves graven images, now falling by the sword, mourning in captivity for the multitude of their transgressions, now bowing their heads to the will of Jehovah, now pouring imprecations upon their enemies, now building and marrying, now destroying, now singing songs of praise, now sacrificing, now comforting, now crucifying their Messiah.

In a book, the making of which has continued from generation to generation, inconsistencies and confusion are inevitable. Yet it is the most important record of the gropings of the human spirit that mankind possesses. Swedenborg set himself the task of separating the dross from the gold, the words of men from the Word of God. He had a genius for interpreting the sacred symbolism of the Bible similar to the genius of Joseph when he revealed the meaning of Pharaoh's dreams in the land of his captivity. The religious leaders of Swedenborg's time darkened counsel with many words without knowledge. While they were helpless before the curtains of God's shrine, Swedenborg drew them aside with subtle insight and revealed the Holy of Holies in all its glory.

CRUEL AND FALSE IDEAS ABOUT GOD

The first and last thought of Swedenborg throughout his theological writings is to show that in the Bible, rightly read and interpreted, is to be found the truest and noblest conception of God possible. Most human minds are so constituted that there is in them a secret chamber where theological subjects are stored, and its center is the idea of God. If this idea is false and cruel, all things that follow it by logical sequence partake of these qualities. For the highest is also the inmost, and it is the very essence of every belief and thought and institution derived from it. This essence, like a soul, forms everything it enters into an image of itself; and as it descends to the planes of daily life, it lays hold of the truths in the mind and infects them with its cruelty and error.

Such was the idea of God in ancient India, where a highly intellectual class attempted to dictate the way of living on the principle that, to be like God, one must crush out all human affection and duties and relations; and the moment one became utterly passionless, without thought or interest in anything external, one was godlike—absorbed into the infinite, and ready for another world.

This was an extreme case; but it illustrates the kind of beliefs that are hostile to humanity. By that I mean beliefs that set up fictitious excellences and encourage devotional feeling; and ceremonies that do not have as their object the good of humanity and that are made substitutes for a righteous, useful life. Such beliefs darken all morality and make it an instrument of a supreme being worshipped indeed with adulation, but in truth repulsive to the good and the wise.

VAGUE IDEAS ABOUT GOD

There is another spiritual danger against which Swedenborg often warns his readers—vagueness of thought about God. He says many times that humble folk think more wisely with all their blunders and superstitions about God, the soul, and immortality than many who have great knowledge but who look into creation and into their own minds and find them empty of Divine Truth. How thrillingly significant the words of Jeremiah (9:42) come back to uphold the groping believer:

> Thus saith the Lord, let not the wise man glory in his wisdom; neither let the mighty man glory in his might; let not the rich man glory in his riches; but let him that glorieth glory in this, that he understandeth and knoweth me, that I am the Lord, who executeth loving-kindness, judgment, and righteousness in the earth, for in these things I delight, saith the Lord.

Love and God are so closely allied that we cannot know much about one and miss the other. God, like love, must be made visible. A wandering idea of an invisible God, Swedenborg declares,

> is not determined to anything; for this reason it ceases and perishes. The idea of God as a spirit, when a spirit is believed to be as ether or wind, is an empty idea; but

the idea of God as Man is a just idea; for God is Divine Love and Divine Wisdom, with every quality belonging to them, and the subject of these is man, and not ether or wind. (*Apocalypse Revealed*, paragraph 224)

Again says Swedenborg:

If anyone thinks of the Divine itself without the idea of Divine Man, he thinks vaguely, and a vague idea is no idea at all; or he conceives an idea of the Divine from the visible universe without a boundary, or which ends in obscurity, which idea makes one with the idea of the worshippers of Nature; it also falls into Nature, and becomes no idea. (*Arcana Coelestia*, paragraph 8705)

And finally:

All who come into heaven have their place alloted them there, and thence eternal joy, *according to their idea of God.* (*Apocalypse Revealed*, paragraph 224, emphasis added)

THE KEY TO UNDERSTANDING SCRIPTURE

When the three-fold nature of the human being—spirit, intellect, and body—is rightly understood, it will be found that all forms one perceives pass into the imagination, and one's soul endows them with life and meaning. Humanity and the universe are pictures in the divine mind. God created human beings in the divine image and likeness. In turn, people send forth into their mind and body and the world thought-forms stamped with their own individuality. It is known how artists see beautiful pictures in their minds before they paint them. Similarly, the spirit projects ideas into thought-images or symbols; that is the universal and the only true language. If one could convey joy or faith or a mental picture of a sunrise to another in visible form, how much more satisfactory that would be than the many words and phrases of ordinary language!

I have cried when I touched an embossed Chinese symbol that represents happiness, and no amount of description would have produced such an effect upon me. It was a picture of a man with his mouth close to a rice field. How forcibly it brought home the fact that the Chinese are utterly dependent upon the rice they grow and that when their fields are flooded and the crops destroyed, starvation for millions of human beings is inevitable.

Many ideas crowded into one symbol gain a power that words tend to neutralize. The French say that "words are employed to conceal ideas." The English author John Ruskin has an eloquent passage in *Sesame and Lilies* where he speaks of words as masks that draw the mind away from real issues to external things.

The Bible is largely written in this universal language. Of course, Christians knew this before Swedenborg's day. They were familiar with its "dark sayings" and parables; but to them, as to most of us, a great many chapters—and the book of Revelation especially—were utterly unintelligible. "Verily, thou art a God that hidest thyself, O God of Israel, the Savior" (Isaiah 45:15), describes exactly the hidden truths of the Word. The children of Israel did not know God, except in the cloud and the pillar of fire and through the rod of his power. When God caused himself to be seen in human form upon earth, he was called an ally of the prince of devils. Even his own disciples mistook his divine purpose and disputed among themselves as to who should be greatest in his kingdom. They misinterpreted his work of love as a plan of conquest and personal glory.

Over all God's ways there is a covering. His very revelation is veiled in the clouds. The Word that professes to show God to us clothes him in the limitations of finite human nature, and we gain the most contradictory impressions of his attributes. God is infinite and eternal, and yet our human passions and ignorance are ascribed to him. God says in Scripture, "Fury is not in me" (Isaiah 27:4) and "I am not angry, you provoke yourselves unto anger" (Jeremiah 7:19), yet God also pours out fierce wrath upon the earth. God is presented as one who "doth not repent" (1 Samuel 15:29), and he does repent. God gives to each person according to their own works, and yet God visits the sins of the previous generation upon its children (cf. Exodus 20:5 and Deuteronomy 24:16). There is a long series of such apparent contradictions, and it is natural that many people cannot see any order underlying such a chaos of irreconcilable ideas. If we believe in a God at all worthy of love, we cannot think of him as angry, capricious, or changeable. It seems as though these conceptions must have been part of the barbarism of the times when the Bible was written.

Swedenborg develops a philosophy of Divine Revelation that is reasonable. He points out that, as in science, every revelation of new ideas from God must be suited to the states and the capacities of those who receive them. He undertakes to show that the literal statement of the Bible is an adaptation of Divine Truth to the minds of people who are very simple or sensuous or perverse. He demonstrates that there is a spiritual sense within the literal verse, suited to the higher intelligence of the angels who also read God's Word and think with us, although they are invisible. In this superior sense is the fullness of Divine Truth.

What would a friend care about what I said to him if he took my words literally? Would I not appear to him mentally unbalanced if he thought I meant to say that the sun rises and sets, or the earth is flat, or that I do not live in the dark? It is the meaning my friend listens to, not the words or the appearances that they convey.

That process is very similar to the method Swedenborg employs in finding the deeper meaning of the Bible. God appears small and undivine if a dull, perhaps bad person reads that God is angry with the wicked every day. But an individual of sense and heart sees that it is only an appearance and that we project onto God our own anger with each other and the punishment we have brought upon ourselves. There is, however, the anger of the just that subsides in a moment and is understood as love that chastens.

God is incapable even of sternness, and he tells his people this over and over again. As we penetrate into his Divine Word, putting aside one covering after another, we come closer to his true nature. He did not create humanity and then betray and reject us from Eden. He does not teach laws and break them and impute guilt to his creatures. He warns but does not cast people into hell or forsake them. It is mankind who constrains God to express commandments in language that can be comprehended and acted upon. The British poet Algernon Charles Swinburne was unconsciously feeling the Divine Presence when he wrote these lines contrasting the difference between "religious duty" and God's love:

> Oh my sons, too dutiful
> Towards gods not of me,

Was I not enough beautiful?
Was it hard to be free?
For behold, I am with you, am in you, and of you;
Look forth now and see.

Who would ever realize the abuse that is piled up to the heavens daily and hurled upon this more than beautiful, all-enduring Deity! He does not really hide himself; but the determined, evil speech of selfishness hides him.

I have said all this because we need to have a very clear, unclouded idea of God's nature if we are to read the symbols of God's Word connectedly. According to this theory, the spiritual sense deals with the soul exclusively—its needs and trials, its changes and renewals, not of times, places, and persons. When we read of mountains, rivers, lambs and doves, thunder and lightning, golden cities and precious stones, and the trees of life with healing leaves, we may know that they are exact symbols of the spiritual principles that lie back of them. Affections and ideas are signified, and their uses to the soul are similar to the uses of their natural representatives to the body.

This rule of interpretation was employed by Swedenborg for twenty-seven years; and at the end of that time, he did not have to change or correct one biblical statement given in his first published work. He gives the same spiritual equivalent for the same natural object throughout the Bible, and the meanings fit wherever they are applied. I know; I have tried this key, and it fits. This is what Swedenborg calls the law of correspondences—analogies between the forms of nature and those of spirit. The Bible may be called the poem of the world as well as God's finite utterance to man.

Swedenborg's works, especially the *Arcana Coelestia* [*Secrets of Heaven*], confirm much of what Robert Ingersoll and other critics of the Bible say about the untrustworthiness of its literal statements; but at the same time, it is demonstrated that they are quite wrong in their conclusions about its value from a different point of view. I have had abundant opportunity to learn how defective the sense of the letter is in the light of modern science, how strange some of the stories are, and how often they lack outward harmony. Nevertheless, I have also observed that there is a meaning beneath the letter that cannot be read in word but only in symbol, and this meaning holds good throughout the parts where it occurs.

There is a compelling example of it in Psalm 78: "I will open my mouth in a parable; I will utter dark sayings of old, which we have heard and known, and our fathers have told us." Then follows in the psalm a summary of the experiences of the Israelites in Egypt and their pilgrimage to Canaan. This record is true history; but here it is pronounced to be a parable that only the initiated can fully grasp. And what a deep parable it is! It describes perfectly our exodus from materialism and ignorance, and our slow, difficult progress toward the happier life, which the beautiful, fertile land of Canaan represents. This is an illustration of how Swedenborg always regards the Bible as a vehicle of divine truth.

ONE VAST, GLORIOUS PARABLE

It is of interest to recall that in 1753 Astruc made his famous discovery of two or more documents in the Pentateuch; and at that very time, Swedenborg was publishing anonymously in London the *Arcana Coelestia*, explaining Genesis and Exodus. Swedenborg did not believe that Scripture had anything to do with the physical creation or a literal deluge or that the first eleven chapters of Genesis were about individuals named Adam and Noah. It was a very different level of the subject that came to his attention. He was enabled by the study of Hebrew and by his mental illumination to see that the early chapters gave an account in ancient parabolical style of the spiritual life of our race from the beginning down to the Judaic era.

He pointed out that the first chapter contains the stages of evolution by which the mind of humanity, at first dark and chaotic, was developed until it reached the Eden of simple truth and happiness. This age continued until self-interest asserted its power and the innocence of childhood was gradually lost. At last wrong ideas flooded the world. Then a keen race of men, denoted by Noah in the ark, began a new age. Intelligence grew rapidly, and the rod of conscience replaced the voice of the pure soul. The symbol was no longer a garden but a vineyard.

Humanity grew up like ambitious youth, building the great empires of the East whose records we are now recovering year by year. The civilization of that period was extensive, but in time it declined. Polytheism and idolatry came into being. War and violence threatened to cover the face of the earth with ruins, and another dispensation had to be established.

That was the beginning of Judaism, which kept monotheism alive until, in the fullness of time, Christianity dawned upon the world. The first Christian civilization was essentially a continuation of the Judaic tradition—full of the rough makeshifts and tallow candles and flickering torches of a faith fitted to a turbulent society. The sense-pictures and fair engravings of ritual and the scepter of authority beheld, as it were, in the margin of the Word were superstitiously revered; but the divine meaning remained unread.

So passed the perverse infancy and adolescence of the world, and we continue to feel its passionate outbreaks and downfalls and unhappy moods. But now the arc light of a more enlightened faith shines upon humanity, and the creation of a new human goes on step by step; yea, the Sabbath of peace in all hearts and in the outer world shall yet come, and the reign of selfish, blind instincts shall vanish forever.

Thus the Bible is portrayed as one vast glorious parable. All the way one may read in it lessons of life and its phases—its first innocence, its youthful waywardness, its saving conversion, and its incalculable possibilities of service and joy. It is a complete circle from paradise to paradise—"the circle of the earth upon which sitteth the Lord forever" (Isaiah 40:22). The limited language and imperfect modes of thought of days long gone by are only the body of a heavenly message that declares God to be always with us, imparting new and higher gifts and capabilities.

THE MEANING OF THE BOOK OF REVELATION

The Lord Jesus Christ is named in the beginning and in the closing sentence of the book of Revelation; he is the central figure of the book. He is the Jesus of the New Testament. Revelation is the sequel to the Gospels, which tell of God's work upon the earth, his crucifixion, and his resurrection. It tells how he has continued his work in the might of his glorified humanity—the supreme example and inspirer. In the Gospels, Jesus said, "Lo, I am with you always, even unto the end of the world" (Matthew 28:20); and he often spoke of the comfort and enlightenment he would yet bring to men.

What has become of this promise? Except for the coming of the Holy Spirit on the day of Pentecost—which gave the disciples the wisdom to teach, as well as courage and joy for a short time—the promise appears to have been quite forgotten.

But Swedenborg shows that Revelation takes up this promise and prophesies its fulfillment. By symbols it pictures the nature of the risen Lord, the blessings that flow from his presence, and tells explicitly what we must do to prepare our minds for him. It gives fully the ideals of Christian life that shine like stars around this glorious presence and that are only faintly outlined by the apostles; it exposes the cruel beliefs and evils of life that must be overcome before these ideals can become a part of ourselves. It shows the chief obstacles to true Christianity—faith without charity and the greed for domination by means of rituals, superstitions, and terror.

The beasts arising out of the sea and the bottomless pit represent such mental monsters as predestination, intellectual bondage, and the idea of three gods, which has divided men's minds and rendered "one-pointed" conduct impossible, as the Hindus would say. For such ideas destroy all power of spiritual concentration, breed unbalanced emotions, tear asunder the texture of ethics, and drive away philosophy, which lives only in the unity of God. The dragon described in Revelation is every effort of unscrupulous people to reason away the divinity of the Lord and the necessity of keeping his commandments. Babylon is all pride and conceit that prevent the acknowledgment of God and a life according to his truth.

Many chapters of Revelation are full of scenes of judgment in the world of spirits. Seals are opened, and trumpets sound, which means that the darkness and hypocrisy of a decadent church are uncovered. Through all the scenes moves God in his divine humanity. The strength of his love, the purity of his wisdom, and the zeal of his providence are symbolized by the golden girdle about his breast, his head like snow, his eyes like flames of fire, and his face shining as the sun in all its glory. His voice like many waters is the spreading of new thoughts and higher beliefs into the systems of the earth.

Swedenborg clearly tells herein why the Lord's presence has been so little felt since the days when he walked upon the earth, beheld by mortal eyes, and why there has been such small comfort from his spirit. Dominion and oppression have robbed him of us, as it were, and the church in past ages has so narrowed education that people now must struggle to grow to the degree of knowledge necessary for a new message from him.

Beyond the scenes of judgment, we see a loving God gladdening heaven and earth with his smile as the New Jerusalem descends—a new dispensation. We read, "The tabernacle of God is with men" (Revelation 21:3), and again, "I saw no temple therein, for the Lord God Almighty and the Lamb are the temple of it" (Revelation 21:22). The Lord's own human nature is the "tabernacle of God with men," the temple of his presence.

Swedenborg interprets the measure of the Holy City—a full, generous measure, the measure of the perfect humanity attained by the Lord while in the world. The waters flowing from the throne of God are abundant and refreshing truths for those who truly unite their lives with his. For the acknowledgment of the divine humanity of God is the wisdom that opens the inexhaustible fountains of truth in Old Testament parables, psalms, and prophecies, in the Gospels, and especially in this long-sealed book of Revelation.

How divinely beautiful it all is when rightly understood! The picture of the seven candlesticks and in the midst of them one like unto the Son of Man stands as the frontispiece of this book and, under the inspired touch of Swedenborg's mind, it grows brighter and richer until it culminates in the vision of the holy city with the river of life and the tree with the leaves of healing for all nations and the sunshine of God's presence, never again to be hidden from his children.

THE FULFILLMENT OF PROPHECY

Swedenborg's two books explaining the book of Revelation are a fulfillment of the age-long prophecy in the mind of every person who sees "the Son of Man coming in the clouds of heaven with power and great glory" (Matthew 23:30). For to "see" is to understand; "the clouds of heaven" are the letter of the Word, and "the Son of Man coming" is the Lord in the power and the glory of the spiritual sense shining through the letter.

Above the cross was placed the inscription "Jesus of Nazareth, King of the Jews" (John 19:19), written in Hebrew, Greek, and Latin. It foreshadowed the time when the Lord would satisfy longing souls with his likeness, revealing the hidden meanings of the Hebrew Word and the Greek New Testament, and giving the Spiritual Sense in Latin. In this language Swedenborg wrote, translating, as God taught him, the symbols of the Bible into principles of practical life for the use and happiness of humanity.

It was his great task to do so, for the church had departed from the simple, direct, and inspiring story of how our Lord came upon earth clothed in visibility and dwelt as a man among men. For the marvelous reality, the clergy substituted fantasies that entangled them in metaphysical webs from which they could not extricate themselves. The beautiful truth of the divine humanity became distorted, disassociated, dissected beyond recognition; and God himself was lost in deadly dialectics.

Swedenborg brought together the scattered and broken parts, gave them normal shape and meaning, and thus established a "new communion with God in Christ." Swedenborg was not a destroyer but a divinely inspired interpreter. He was a prophet sent by God. His own message proclaims it more convincingly than any of his followers could. As we read his works, we are filled with recognition and delight. He did not make a new Bible, but he made the Bible all new.

REVOLUTIONARY IDEAS

*I, even I, am the Lord, And besides me
there is no savior.* (Isaiah 43:11)

THERE IS ONLY ONE GOD

Guided by the light of the Divine Word, Swedenborg saw the oneness of God in person and essence, and Jesus as God in the humanity that he assumed on earth, and the Holy Spirit as the infinite power for creating goodness and happiness. Jehovah wrought the most stupendous act in earth's history as gently and unobtrusively as he pours his light upon mind and nature. One of the infallible tokens of divinity is its perfect quietness and self-effacement. When God "finited" himself, as it were, and became a little child, there was no glory, except a light on the hills where the shepherds heard the angels sing and a star in the east. There was not even a man of perfect form and stature: only a little babe lying in a manger.

He was apparently just like any other child. His growth, mental and physical, was normal, and as we follow the story of his life, we find him a man among men, earning his daily bread as they did, walking with them along the seashore and by the hillside paths. Yet he was called Immanuel, which means "God with us" (Matthew 1:23).

This truth is the center of Christian teaching; and unless this is perceived clearly, the Bible cannot be rationally explained. In this way we can joyously cherish the one God without denying but rather infinitely exalting Jesus Christ—that beautiful personality toward whom millions of hearts have yearned during the ages.

> And all must love the human form,
> In heathen, Turk, or Jew:
> Where Mercy, Love, and Pity dwell
> There God is dwelling too.
> (WILLIAM BLAKE, "THE DIVINE IMAGE")

The joy inspired by such a concept of God is like the sun with its threefold glory of warmth, light, and activity. It is like the satisfaction with which one beholds the happy balance of soul, mind, and body in a beautiful human being, or the perfect sequence of seed sprouting into blossom, and the blossom yielding luscious fruit.

How sane and easy and capable of fitting into the nature of all things such a concept is! Yet what prodigious effort it cost Swedenborg to plant it so that it could grow and flourish! He uprooted vast encumbrances of argument and conjecture on the trinity and justification by faith alone, just as Francis Bacon substituted direct observation of nature for the scholastic method of deductive reasoning. They both obeyed the call of everlasting truth, committed themselves to the difficulties and the solitude of a new era, and upheld their opinions against the hostility of the public with hope that they might provide a guidance more faithful and secure for coming generations.

GOD'S GOODNESS IS INFINITE

The new thoughts about the unity of God that Swedenborg offered as replacement for the old concepts are precious because they give one the insight to distinguish between the real Deity and the repelling appearance that results from a wrong reading of the Word as well as from the anthropomorphic attributes with which passion-driven men have invested him. The following extract from *True Christian Religion* (paragraph 56) shows how Swedenborg strove to supplant those unchristian concepts with a nobler faith:

> God is omnipotent, because He has all power from Himself, and all others have power from Him. His power and will are one, and because He wills nothing but what is good, therefore He can do nothing but what is good. In the spiritual world, no one can do anything contrary to his own will; this they derive there from God whose power and will are one. God also is good itself; therefore, while He does good, He is in Himself and cannot go out of Himself. From this it is manifest that His omnipotence proceeds and operates within the sphere of the extension of good, which is infinite; for this sphere fills the universe and everything in it.
>
> It may be evident how delirious they are who think, still more they who believe, and yet more they who teach,

that God can condemn anyone, curse anyone, cast anyone into hell, predestine the soul of anyone to eternal death, avenge injuries, be angry, or punish. On the contrary, He is not able to turn away from anyone, or look at anyone with a stern countenance.

Such teachings lift one up to a mountain summit where the atmosphere is clear of hatred, and one can perceive that the nature of God is love and wisdom and use and that he never changes his attitude toward anyone at any time.

THE OLD VIEW

The higher criticism of the Bible, as Swedenborg indicates, does not take away a jot or tittle of its essential meaning but corrects erroneous views of the early Hebrew writers. In this view, then, there is no conflict with the accumulating data of archaeology, and geology, and the study of different documents. The Bible is lifted to a higher level than ever before and is clothed with holiness.

The old view was most unworthy of the great God of all souls. He was supposed to have said nothing until Sinai. He had left no room for science to work without making trouble for faith. His instruction of the race had been through the narrow and exclusive ray of light to Moses. His providences were chiefly heartless neglects. All nations except Israel were under his ban, and millions must have been swept into the abyss. Then his "beloved Son" interceded, and offered himself up as a sacrifice upon the cross for an otherwise doomed race; then the "Father" was propitiated, and cancelled his sentence—but only for persons in whose behalf the "Son" spoke a good word!

This old view was Swedenborg's arch enemy; for it was constantly taught in the schools, preached and proclaimed with the utmost zeal and eloquence. Its gigantic shadow lay on the baby's cradle and brooded over the prison and the deathbed; it has penetrated even the smallest acts and common sayings of every day. Skeptics and atheists naturally sprang up everywhere. Faith in God and in his Word seemed to demand the suppression of science and philosophy and the smothering of all generous sentiments.

THE NEW VIEW

Swedenborg confronted this giant with a new view that brought fresh hope and appreciation of the Bible. The God he followed is the God of all nations and all times. Infinitely patient and unselfish, he has watched over the whole world. At first he led childlike humanity by the same law of spontaneous growth by which he forms a beautiful tree; then he taught people in the parables of garden, flood, vineyard, and tower; and afterward in the books of Moses and the Prophets.

There have always been laws of justice in every land. But the Ten Commandments were given at Sinai in a special manner, so that they might include all the spiritual laws that wisdom and science would reveal as the centuries passed.

Whenever the Jews turned aside from this sacred trust for all men—the Ten Commandments—they were rebuked pointedly with the example of many other people who did not have the Word in writing but upon whose wise and noble minds the Truth was inscribed as with letters of gold. Swedenborg holds up many of the non-Christians of his day as examples of sincerity and well-doing that should put Christendom to shame, and lo! now it is they who are showing the most determined courage for the cause of brotherhood, while we devise more effective ways to kill one another in the next war. Truly, the Word of God stands forever, though the old heaven and earth of literalism melt away.

I had been told by narrow people that all who were not Christians would be punished, and naturally my soul revolted, since I knew of wonderful men who had lived and died for truth as they saw it in the pagan lands. But when I read Swedenborg's *Heaven and Hell*, I found that "Jesus" stands for Divine Good, good wrought into deeds, and "Christ" symbolizes Divine Truth, sending forth new thought, new life, and joy into the minds of all people; therefore, no one who believes in God and lives right is ever condemned.

We are beginning to perceive the Divine Providence as Swedenborg describes it—in a circle of large, noble ideas that are consistent with its greatness. Previously, it was darkened by controversial dogmas, and often its meaning has degenerated into special provisions that imply special neglects. But in Swedenborg's teaching it is shown to be the government of God's love and wisdom and the creation of uses. Since God's life cannot be less in one being than another, or his love manifested less fully in one thing than another, his providence must be universal.

The idea that vast multitudes are excluded from the blessings of salvation through Jesus Christ is giving way to a more generous understanding that God has "other sheep who hear his voice and obey him" (John 10:16). He has provided religion of some kind everywhere, and it does not matter to what race or creed people belong if they are faithful to their ideals of right living.

The one principle to be remembered by all is that religion is to live a doctrine, not merely to believe one.

It was of the Divine Providence that Muhammed arose to overthrow idol worship. This great prophet taught a form of religion adapted to the Arab mind and temperament, which explains the mighty influence for good this faith has exercised in many empires and kingdoms. The history of religious thought proclaims in trumpet tones that God has never left himself without a witness.

If we view the Divine Providence from the heaven in our minds, past experiences yield up to us precious lessons of wisdom and helpfulness, and we feel the harmony of life. But if we look at God's ways from a world of accident, chance, and discord, we misunderstand them utterly. We regard him as an arbitrary dispenser of rewards and punishments, partial to favorites and vengeful to adversaries. We presume upon his immensity with our petty patriotisms and pray to him for victory. We turn to warring sects—and where is he? It has even been said to me, "If there were a God, would he not have created people so that they could never sin?" As if anybody wished people to be automatons! Not to be able to sin could satisfy only a despot; does not the spirit shiver at such a concept? In fact, all denials of God are found at last to be denials of freedom and humanity.

The living value of a belief depends not on our own limited experience but on its benefit to mankind; and an overruling beneficence is the only teaching that ultimately justifies our knowledge or gives dignity to civilization.

Wherever, as is the tendency of conventional worship, the dogmas of a nation turn wicked, simple good people abound who remain unharmed by them because they are far from the corruption in high places. Beneficence includes many gifts, but above all the power of going out of oneself and appreciating whatever is noble in man and wonderful in the universe. As Swedenborg put it, "Good is like a little flame which gives light, and causes man to see, perceive, and believe" (*Arcana Coelestia*, paragraph 5816:2).

WHAT DOES IT MEAN TO BE "BORN AGAIN"?

Another concept, revolutionary in those days, is that there is no such thing as predestination to hell. All are born for heaven, as the seed is born to become a flower and the little thrush in the nest is intended to become a song-bird—if the laws of life are obeyed. In other words, all have been redeemed, and all can be regenerated, and it is our own fault if we live and think ourselves out of heaven. But we go there every time we think a noble thought; and we stay there when it has become our happiness to serve others.

Swedenborg's teachings about life can best be understood if we carefully differentiate between life and existence. God bestows existence upon each of us for the express purpose of imparting life to us. His infinite love impels him to be a creator, since love must have objects to which it can give its wealth of good-will and beneficence. In the love which is the life of God, we find the origin of creation. His infinite will cannot be satisfied with anything less than the existence of beings who can be finite recipients of his own happiness. At the same time, such beings must have freedom and the rationality that accompanies true freedom. That is, his gift of life to us must be received

All are born for heaven, as the seed is born to become a flower
and the little thrush in the nest is intended to become a song-bird.

voluntarily and thoughtfully if it is to become our own. That is why we pass through two distinct experiences—the birth into existence and the birth into life.

When we are born of the flesh, we are utterly helpless and dependent, while in the spiritual birth we are active and in a sense co-creators. We have nothing to do with our birth into existence; for we must exist before we can make anything of ourselves. On the other hand, our birth into life is a matter of choice: we have a very direct share in it, for no real spiritual life can be thrust upon us against our will.

This is the meaning of God's constant, loving invitation through his Word to all of us—to come unto him and choose life, and be ever on our guard against the evils that would rob us of the life that we have chosen. Only by exercising our powers of thought and keeping our hearts always warm and pure do we become truly alive. But this beautiful work of re-creation comes not by observation; it is wrought in the quiet depths of the soul. For, as the Lord says, "The wind bloweth where it listeth, and thou hearest the sound thereof, but thou canst not tell whence it cometh and whither it goeth; so is everyone that is born of the spirit" (John 3:8).

We should not think, therefore, of conversion as the acceptance of a particular creed, but as a change of heart. It is the soul turning away from the ignoble instincts that tempt us to feel, think, speak, and act for mere self-interest and the good opinion of the world, and finding joy in the unselfish love of God and a life of usefulness to others above all things. Our choice of life is this delight—this sweet expansion of mind and heart without which no worthwhile achievement is possible.

But we are not born again suddenly, as some people seem to think. It is a change that comes over us as we hope and aspire and persevere in the way of the Divine Commandments. For a long time we may resolve like angels, but then we drop back into the old, matter-of-fact way of life and do just what we did before, like mortals. We are already on the road to success, however, when we see that simply because we have always done something, or because everybody does it, or because our grandparents did it that way, this does not mean we should continue to do it. There is no plane of experience where, if we want to, we cannot enlarge our lives by caring about people outside ourselves and seeking the highest, most helpful ideas of him who is "the Way, the Truth, and the Life" (John 14:6). When once we make up our minds to do this and set out fearlessly, all outward circumstances and limitations give way before us. We take up our cross daily with a stronger heart and a fairer prospect of life and happiness.

SPIRITUAL REGENERATION

Swedenborg's own mind expanded slowly to the higher light, and with deep suffering. The theological systems of his day were little more than controversies, so full of long-drawn-out hair-splittings that they seemed like caverns in which one would easily get lost and never find one's way out again. Swedenborg had to define important keywords, such as *truth*, *soul*, *will*, *state*, and *faith*, and give new meanings to many other words so that he might translate more of spiritual thought into common language. Rather than using terms such as *born again* or *instantaneous salvation*, he spoke of spiritual growth as *regeneration*.

A very real regeneration comes with the change that begins in us when we become conscious of our spiritual faculties. Such a change takes place not only after periods of bereavement and sorrow, but often after experiences of which we alone may be aware. There comes a day when our eyes are cleared, and we see ourselves, our present environment, and the future in their true relations. The scales of selfishness fall away, and we look at our own life soberly.

It is amazing how prodigiously people have written and talked about regeneration, and yet how little has been said to the purpose. Self-culture has been loudly and boastfully proclaimed as sufficient for all our ideals of perfection. But if we listen to the best men and women everywhere, they will answer with a decided negative. Some of them have amassed vast treasures of knowledge, and they will say that science may have found a cure for most evils; but it has found no remedy for the worst of them all—the apathy of human beings. It is pointed out, and Swedenborg says the same thing, that humanity, unschooled in love and pity, is worse than a beast. It is a hornless tailless, animal; it does not eat grass, but it wantonly destroys with its reckless power of thought. We invent more and more horrible weapons to kill and mar our brothers and sisters in war; we mutilate helpless animals for sport or for the changing whims of fashion; and we have a passion for faultfinding and scandal that rises beyond control. Many other evils are no doubt traceable to human ignorance, but certainly not these pernicious tendencies. Our deliverance is not going to be through self-culture unaided by right desires.

There is another large group of well-meaning people who hold that we can be reformed largely by a change of environment; and there is enough truth in this to render it plausible and attractive. But it is overemphasized and often wrongly applied. It is not environment that alters a human being, but forces within the individual. The blind, the deaf, the prisoner for conscience's sake, even the poorest men and women with sound ideals have all proved that they can shape life nearer to their desires, no matter what the outward circumstance.

Because there is a good deal of the child in us, we grow impatient easily and say to ourselves, "Oh if we could stand in the lot of our more fortunate neighbors, we could live better, happier, and more useful lives." How often we hear a young person say, "If I had the opportunity of my boss's son, I could achieve great success." "If I didn't have to associate with such vulgar folk, I could become morally strong," says another, and a third laments, "If I only had the money of my wealthy friend, I should gladly do my part in the uplift of the world."

Now, I am as much up in arms against needless poverty and degrading influences as anyone else; but at the same time, I believe human experience teaches that if we cannot succeed in our present position, we could not succeed in any other. Unless, like the lily, we can rise pure and strong above sordid surroundings, we would probably be moral weaklings in any situation. Unless we can help the world where we are, we could not help it if we were somewhere else. The most important issue is not the sort of environment we have, but the kind of thoughts we think every day, the kind of ideals we are following—in a word, the kind of men and women we really are. The Arab proverb is admirably true: "That is thy world wherein thou findest thyself."

Swedenborg has all these different theories in mind when he makes it clear that human beings cannot be regenerated suddenly without doing terrible violence to their minds and their self-esteem. They must advance step by step, accustoming their inner eyes to a keener light before they can endure the dazzle of new truths, and they cannot be turned toward a good life except by their delights. For it is these delights that keep them free and at last give them the power to choose.

Cooperation with God, confidence in his unwearying help, learning to understand more truths in the Word, living according to them, and doing good for its own sake—these are the only wholesome ways for mortals to rise out of their old selves and rebuild their world. They are greatly to be pitied if they wish to steal the merits of Christ or demand heaven as a "reward." It is much nobler for them to look into their own hearts and drive out the dragon of selfishness; this repentance they can accomplish quickly, but they must grow slowly and as cheerfully as possible, or they will never acquire any abiding strength of character. Those who rise in this manner will never stop regenerating in this life or the next, since they will forever find more to love, more to know, more to achieve.

Swedenborg's *Divine Providence* powerfully elucidates the truth that God created the universe because of his infinite need to give life and joy. The futility and hollowness of belief in a remote, unapproachable deity is shown in many a passage of that comforting work. Swedenborg writes that "the Lord's divine providence has for its object a heaven from the human race and the conjunction of mankind with Himself" (paragraph 44). Elsewhere he declares that "it is the essence of God's love to love others, to desire to be one with them, and from Himself to make them happy" (*True Christian Religion*, paragraph 43). That is the whole of the Divine Providence, and we must let ourselves be borne along by it as by a current if we wish to accomplish our part in God's work of spiritual rehabilitation.

In the vicissitudes of our lives, therefore, the Divine Providence looks not to temporal blessings only, but chiefly to our eternal welfare and happiness. The million little things that drop into our hands, the small opportunities that each day brings, God leaves us free to use or abuse—and goes unchanging along his silent way. Yet always he guards the right of everyone to act in freedom according to reason; for liberty and rationality are his primary means for the regeneration of mankind and tokens of his gift of immortality.

OUR NOBLER NATURE

Since we are all too prone to live selfishly, it is necessary that there should be something within us to offset this tendency. The choice of a better life that we are to make involves some previous knowledge of such a life. What could save us from becoming more and more like animals if there were not present within us other tendencies of a nobler kind? We cannot freely and wisely choose the right way for ourselves unless we know both good and evil.

This is all said to explain Swedenborg's doctrine of *reliquiae* as a powerful factor in molding life. That word, often translated as "remains," signifies the lasting impressions of love and truth and beauty left in us from the days of our childhood. Only by having definite pictures of heavenly life stamped upon our memories can we learn to imagine more beautiful ones and make them living realities.

According to this teaching, at birth we are passive. Our inherited evil tendencies are as yet quiescent. That is why little children are so near to heaven, and we so often feel that the angels are ministering to them. "Their angels do always behold the face of my Father which is in heaven" (Matthew 18:10). Truly, children come in "trailing clouds of glory," each with characteristics and potentialities different from any other human being. They receive capabilities of goodness and wisdom from God alone, and in a very real sense, heaven enspheres them like the sunshine.

This is the way Swedenborg accounts for the beautiful innocence and trust of the little child. We never completely lose this innocence and trust. Our stored-up capabilities (*reliquiae*) are the holy places where we feel our kinship with the Divine. These are the places of sacrifice, the meeting-ground of mortal and immortal, the tents of trial where are waged the great spiritual combats of human life. Here are the tears and agonies and the bloody sweat of Gethsemane. Here, too, is the victory. Here is the shrine of life we have chosen.

SECRETS OF THE SPIRITUAL WORLD

*Truly, I say to you, today you will
be with me in Paradise.* (Luke 23:43)

IN OUR FATHER'S HOUSE

Swedenborg's revelations take from every grave its fear. Before his work was known, the future life was, for most Christians, full of terrors. It was a disputed question whether life or death brought greater opportunity—whether death was the end of life or the door to another existence.

Now we are positive that the larger, nobler life is beyond the grave. It used to be that a child dying in his mother's arms was an intolerable thought. Now we know of the sweet, unclouded childhood that awaits all children who die in infancy. We know that in our Father's house, angels will teach them to speak, think creative thoughts, and do the work for which they are best fitted, where they will grow in beauty and go forth to deeds and adventures mightier than were ever beheld upon earth. We know now that every faithful love that has been thwarted here has tenfold greater joy in store for it on the other side. This is the meaning behind those beautiful words, "Let not your heart be troubled . . . in my Father's house there are many mansions" (John 14:1,2).

FRIENDSHIPS IN HEAVEN

According to all of Swedenborg's testimony, after death we are like travelers going from place to place, becoming acquainted with all kinds of interesting objects, meeting all sorts of people and receiving something from each individual on the way. We observe, judge, criticize, and listen to words of wisdom or folly. We drop an opinion, take up another, sift it, and test it in our mental crucible. From each new experience we extract finer kinds of knowledge and those truer intellectual concepts that are the property of all. On earth we live apart, though not alone, and the most wonderful of our thoughts, due to lack of listeners, has never been uttered.

But in the other life it is different. All live together and learn together. All spirit beings, good and bad, are minds, and they communicate to each other instantly volumes of ideas that would require long periods to comprehend upon earth. So we journey onward, choosing the comrades best suited to us, and grow increasingly interested, wiser, saner, nobler, and happier through all eternity. What a prospect this opens up to those whose spirit wings are fettered by the uninspired and limited facts of mortality! What an inexpressible comfort to those who hunger for lofty friendship and living communion!

I believe that in heaven friendships may endure, as indeed they do on earth, by changing as well as by their steadfastness. For it is their nature to vitalize and diversify the ideas and emotions that enter the field of consciousness. Here on earth we are inclined to lay stress on likeness and ignore difference; but in heaven, and sometimes here among us, too, friends similar in spirit are so different they offset or complement each other like varied and beautiful colors in the sunrise. They discover each other and give and receive the best that is in them. They do for each other's souls what our acquaintances do when they feed and clothe our bodies.

A feeling of amazement comes over me as I realize how fully I know this from experience. I am the happy object of a rare friendship that makes my teacher a seer of the capabilities folded away in me that darkness and silence would hide from most people. There are moments in our lives so lovely they transcend earth and anticipate heaven for us. This foretaste of eternity has made clear to me the perpetual and all-embracing service that friendship should be.

WHAT DO PEOPLE DO IN HEAVEN?

The Bible says that in heaven we "rest from our labors" (Revelation 14:13); but that only means that when we have worked out our salvation through sorrow, failure, and temptation, we reach the sabbath of peace and innocence. The "labors" we rest from are the obstacles of the flesh; the struggle for bread, clothing, and shelter; war; and the sordid schemes to outdo each other for gain or power. But immense fields of glorious work and endless interest await all of us who are faithful over a few tasks here.

Occupations in the kingdom of uses, as heaven is called, cannot be enumerated or described specifically, for they are infinitely varied. Those with unselfish parental love adopt and take care of little ones from earth. Some educate boys and girls;

others give instruction to the simple and earnest who desire it. Again, all people of every religion are taught new truths to enlarge and refine their limited beliefs. There are special societies to care for everyone who rises through death into life, to defend newcomers to the spiritual world against the unfriendliness of evil spirits, to keep guard over those who inhabit hell and prevent them from tormenting each other beyond endurance, and thus to lessen their sense of misery as far as may be possible.

Since all human beings live both in this natural world and in the spiritual realm at the same time, angels from every society are chosen to guard mortals, to diminish little by little their lusts and wrong habits of thought and tenderly turn their love of dark deeds into the joy of deeds of light. Only unwillingness in the human heart ever restrains the loving ministries of these angels and, even then they keep returning with steadfast faith and patience, for they are images and messengers of Divine Fidelity. They scarcely see, and even less dwell upon, anyone's faults, but instead they study all that person's beauties of disposition and mind, and interpret evil into good.

By focusing on their God-given talent, men and women who are becoming angels rise continually to nobler tasks; and each new state brings them an influx of new powers, which is what is meant by God's promise of "full measure, shaken down, pressed together, and running over" (Luke 6:38). The golden harps and the singing of endless praises, which have raised so much adverse comment and given such an unfavorable impression of lazy saints, are pictorial appearances. They symbolize the heart playing softly on its lyre of joy and singing as the task at hand grows ever more beautiful and satisfying. In heaven we shall

God is Light

Helen Keller

All human beings live both in this natural world
and in the spiritual realm at the same time.

find the beauty and strength of men and women, selfless love between the sexes, the frolic of children, the joys of companionship, and the vital power of touch exquisitely soothing and eloquent. So, in the light of Swedenborg's teachings, heavenly life is a truly human life, and there are all kinds of service—domestic, civil, social, and inspirational—to be performed and enjoyed.

We are also informed that there are three kinds of angels— those whose chief interest is knowledge and the practical work that protects the outposts of heaven against the intrusions of hell, those who philosophize and originate new ideas, and, finally, those who do not need to reason things out because they can empathize with another by their powers of perception and then act directly and quickly. This kind of spontaneity might be compared with the fig tree, which does not stop to blossom, but brings forth its leaves and fruit at the same time.

THE ETERNAL LIFE OF USE

In heaven no one is quite like another, and thus there are innumerable groupings or societies; but there is only one heaven— or heaven is one, just as the human body is one, though composed of countless organs, blood vessels, nerves, and fibers. All lesser ends are subordinated to the common good. In a word, every glory, every ideal, every high desire—all that the dreams of noblest minds have ever whispered, and infinitely more unthought-of possibilities—become substantial realities in the eternal sunshine of immortality.

Science teaches us that each part of the body exists for the benefit of every other part. God breathes a similar purpose into nature. The mineral kingdom is united and serves as a support for the vegetable. The vegetable gives life to us, and thus both mineral and vegetable minister to humanity. This law of benefit, from each to all and all to each, is meant to rule in human life. Many have perverted it and live on the labor and the brains of others; but sooner or later retribution overtakes them, and they must lay their offering of service on the altar of the common good or drop out of the ranks of worthy humanity. This service may be rendered in any of three ways: by the hand, by the intellect, or by our emotional and aesthetic capacities.

Of course, if we view humanity subjectively, the case may be different. We may corrupt our use by selfishness; but the fact remains that, objectively, our whole life and its environment teach the law of use and are the best possible means for us to realize our proper ideals. It is for us to learn how to use that law as our guide. We should seek ways to render it possible for each one of us to select the special activity that shall bring interest and satisfaction and also harmonize with the good of all the rest. Then each of us would find our place in the eternal life of use; this is the only right method of living in this or any other world.

THE PURPOSE OF EDUCATION IN HEAVEN

If it is true that Swedenborg brings a clear, authoritative revelation of heavenly life as it can be best understood—free from all material limitations—we should have a definite idea of the purpose of education there. The heavenly world is a vast realm of souls clothed with spiritual bodies, all interrelated and bound together in one magnificent system. There is not a single individual in all that multitude who has not capabilities, interests, and knowledge of special kinds that facilitate the individual's own higher development and thereby the greater good of all. Depending one upon another, they grow more perfect in their own way and become more responsive to the happiness that is increasingly bestowed upon them.

The type of education we need, and the one that thoughtful people now urge, is that which will help us to appreciate the law of use, to adapt it to ourselves, and to choose the work by which we can best fulfill it. We need a system of education that will teach us about all the varieties of use that surround us and show us the difference between the practical, the mental, and the spiritual services we can render, and one that may impel us to choose the tasks to which our interest and fitness draw us most strongly.

The reason Swedenborg keeps holding up heavenly life as a pattern is that it serves as an object lesson. The old thought tells us we are given earth to prepare for heaven, but there is truth in seeing it the other way around. We are given a knowledge of heaven to fit us better for earth. The Vision of Beauty must come into the workshop of Nazareth. So I do not hesitate to point to what Swedenborg says about the education of children in heaven as a suggestion for our earthly schools. There they are taught largely by "representations"—pictures, instructive plays, and scenery—that is, by illustration and example. They are led to choose the uses they like best and are educated for them.

A MERCIFUL HELL

Some have said that Darwin made a laughingstock of heaven and hell; but they are made no laughingstock in Swedenborg's writings, and they never should be from anyone else's point of view, so long as people are capable of sinning and feeling remorse. We are taught there is no hell of the medieval kind; but there is a mental hell into which people go who are self-confirmed lovers of evil and who willingly deny God in their heart. They do not fall into literal fire, and as they punish themselves more than enough, God takes away from them even the anguish of conscience. That is why they are never forced to put themselves into states of heavenly feeling—they would only be suffocated and robbed of the only pleasures they have. But they "burn" with selfish instincts and the love of dominating others.

They see as they think—like owls and bats. They debate and litigate and fight; they practice endless arts of magic and deception; they must labor hard for air and food, and some of them seem always to be cutting wood and mowing grass because on earth they worked so furiously for rewards. Misers hug to their hearts imaginary moneybags. Sirens try painfully to beautify their pitiful forms and enjoy their images reflected in the dull light, like that of a charcoal fire. Each gang of crooks strives to outwit all the rest, and the fierce joy of rivalry shines luridly on their marred faces. Those who have held tenaciously to their cruel, stupid opinions talk hour after hour to their own idiotic kind and to dumb spirits. When they are weary of their futile efforts, all the genii, gnomes, enchanters, and robbers take hands and dance, like the crazy fantasies of a fevered dream.

But these unfortunate beings are not left useless or despised by God. He brings them into external order and, as far as they can be led by their own affections, he induces them to be of service to others. They enable us to see the evil to be avoided as well as the good we are to choose. They keep alive the fires of ambition in those of us who do not care about ideals or the public welfare, but desire rather fame and honor. They sharpen our minds for the unpleasant truths that we, as children of light, must surely learn if we are to help guard humanity against brute force and oppression, whether it be by one or by many.

It is not God but people who cast themselves into hell. And that hell is selfishness. It was the German mystic Jacob Boehme who called the gnawing, burning appetites and desires of the selfish "the dark worm of hell," of which the Scripture says, "their worm dieth not, and their fire is not quenched" (Mark 9:48).

HOPE FOR THE FUTURE

Heaven and hell have become facts in our deeper consciousness about which there can be no dispute. We have an intuitive certainty of them—not a halting knowledge inferred from arguments or reasons that we can accept or reject as we choose. Swedenborg shows that the state we enter after death is wrought of our own motives, thoughts, and deeds. Only such face-to-face knowledge as he provides gives reality to the things of spirit, since it springs from life-experience.

The difficulty mortals have in believing this arises not so much from the unprovableness of it as from our own incredulous attitude. We believe that only material things are real, and our egotistic desires tend to overwhelm our spiritual strivings and keep our inner faculties from reaching conscious experience. Unable to realize the pernicious influence of acquisitiveness upon human character, we do not understand the true significance of our own spiritual being. Our civilization is a failure in the degree to which our materialism and selfishness make us indifferent to the teachings of philosophers like Swedenborg and to the visions of the great thinkers of the world.

With thoughts as wide as the universe and with scientific precision, Swedenborg tells how angels led him from realm to realm of the spiritual world, showed him the life that comes after death and the reality of things immortal. Angels were his teachers, his guides. He lodged his soul in heaven; he sensed the magnitude of the Divine Providence, the tremendous circumstance of life eternal. He was permitted to walk the winding course of stars and to return to earth with wisdom in his hands. His living testimony will shed an ever-increasing light upon the dark hinterland of our personal soul-experience and reinforce our groping efforts with the daring of immortal purpose.

Swedenborg makes the future life not only conceivable but desirable. His message to the living, who meet death with its attendant separation and sorrow, sweeps across the heart of humanity like some sweet breath from God's presence. We can now meet death as nature does, in a blaze of glory, marching to the grave with a cheerful step, wearing our brightest thoughts and most brilliant anticipations, as nature arrays herself in garments of gold, emerald, and scarlet, as if defying death to rob her of immortality.

For a life in the dark, love is the surest guide.

GOSPEL OF LOVE

God is love, and he who abides in love
abides in God, and God in him. (1 John 4:16)

CHRISTIANITY: THE SCIENCE OF LOVE

Religion has been defined as the science of our relations to God and to our fellow men and what we owe to ourselves. Surely Christianity, rightly understood, is the science of love. When the Lord dwelt upon earth, visible to mortals, he declared that on the two commandments, love of God and love of one's neighbor, "hang all the law and the prophets" (Matthew 22:40).

Who could know the Scriptures, and all human thought for that matter, as profoundly as did the gentle Nazarene charged with his divine mission? His authority is clearly established in the Gospels: "This is life eternal, that they may know thee, the only true God, and Jesus Christ, whom thou hast sent" (John 17:3). It was Jesus who said, "I am the Way, the Truth, and the Life" (John 14:6) and "Seek ye first the kingdom of God and his righteousness and all these things [happiness and material blessings] will be added unto you" (Matthew 6:33). Speaking with the highest authority, Jesus emphasized the divine necessity of love throughout the Gospels. "God is love! God is love! God is love!" was the invariable meaning of such phrases as these: "Love ye one another as I have loved you" (John 13:33) and "If you love me, keep my commandments" (John 14:5).

Jesus always visualized hatred as the opposite of God in every detail, great or small, and his teaching about hell was not that it is a punishment by God, but that hell is the result of the inevitable law that evil recoils upon those who cast themselves into hate and the burning lust and cruel miseries of wounded pride and thwarted egotism.

No matter from what angle Jesus started, he came back to this fact, that he entrusted the reconstruction of the world, not to wealth or caste or power or learning, but to the better instincts of the human race—to the nobler ideals and sentiments of people—to love, which is the mover of the will and the dynamic force of action. He turned his words every conceivable way and did every possible work to convince doubters that love—good or evil—is the life of their life, the fuel of their thoughts, the breath of their nostrils, their heaven or their destruction. There was no exception or modification whatever in his holy, awesome, supreme Gospel of Love.

A BRIEF HISTORY OF LOVE

For two thousand years, so-called believers have repeated "God is Love" without sensing the universe of truth contained in these three momentous words or feeling their stimulating power. As a matter of fact, ever since men began to seriously philosophize about life, there has been a sinister silence on this noblest of all subjects. The history of love as a doctrine is a revelation of the tragedy of how God comes to each of us, to reveal his nature to us, and yet we do not know him: "He was in the world and the world was made through him, and the world did not know him" (John 1:10).

In the fifth century B.C., Empedocles, the Greek philosopher and physician, took credit for being the first to understand the nature of love and to recognize its true place in human affairs. He was trying to find the elements of which the world was composed, and by what processes it was held together. In his list of elements he named *Fire, Water, Earth,* and *Air,* and then went on to include *Love,* saying,

> and Love among them, their equal in length and breadth, her do thou fix in mental vision, nor sit with dazed eyes. She it is who is also thought to be implanted in the mortal members, making them think kindly thoughts and do friendly deeds. They call her Joy and Aphrodite. Her has no mortal yet observed among the elements of the world.

A century afterward, in the most brilliant period of philosophy in Greece, Plato's soul was kindled to generous indignation by Empedocles's words, and with a burst of eloquence he protested against the heartlessness of the wisdom of his age:

> What a strange thing it is that whereas other gods have poems and hymns made in their honor, the great and glorious god Love has no encomiast! The wise have descanted in prose on the virtues of Hercules and other heroes, and have even made the utility of salt the theme of eloquent discourse, and only to think

that there should have been an eager interest created about such things, and yet to this day no one has ever yet dared worthily to hymn Love's praises, so entirely has this great deity been neglected.

I think it was in his discourse on courage, *Lachesis,* that Plato said that to injure anyone, even the most despised slave, was an affront to the holy bond that united gods, men, and things in friendship.

Then, except for the voice of Divine Love speaking its message to the hate-dulled ears of men, more than twenty centuries passed with only here and there a mind brave enough to hear those heavenly communications and attempt to translate them into the harsh speech of earth. St. Augustine, Thomas Aquinas, Thomas à Kempis (whose *Meditations* I have read with joy), Baruch Spinoza, Jacob Boehme, and other mystics stood valiantly on the outskirts of their time and gazed deeply into the vast, unknown sea of feeling that rolls forever beneath the darkness of words not understood. They had penetrating insight into the ways and works of love—the love of God, love of others, and love of self.

Only when Swedenborg arose out of the cold age of reason called the eighteenth century did love as a doctrine again shine forth as the center and life, the beauty and the preserver of all things. With the Bible for his authority, he developed this doctrine to some extent in his *Arcana Coelestia* and more completely and systematically in his *Divine Love and Wisdom.* He interpreted the whole world of human experience in terms of love—the states of love; the activities, powers, and functions of love; the constructive, protective, and courage-stirring dictates of love.

Moreover, the seer discovered that love in the eminent sense is identical with the Divine itself, "that the Lord flows into every angel, every spirit, and every person" (*Arcana Coelestia*, paragraph 6058), that the material universe is God's love wrought into forms suitable to the uses of life, and that the Word of God, rightly understood, reveals the fullness and the wonder of his love toward all the children of humankind. Thus at last a faint ray, traveling through infinity from the Divine Soul, reached the mind of deaf, blind humanity, and lo, the second coming of the Lord was at hand!

A SEER AMIDST THE BLIND

For his doctrine of love, Swedenborg had to find a special vocabulary; indeed, it almost seemed as if he were himself learning a different language. He was baffled by habits of thought that people accustomed to depending largely on their senses would require great courage to change, so firmly are they entrenched in the sense. It was one thing for him to perceive as through a glass, darkly, the spiritual forces that sustain life and quite another thing for him to trace them clearly back to their beautiful origin in God's heart of love and then communicate them to an age of cold reason, disputing creeds, and skeptical inquiry.

The only way I know to give any idea of what Swedenborg was up against is to suggest the tremendous obstacles blind people encounter when they wish to help other handicapped people. They must spend their lives trying to make the seeing understand the particular needs of the sightless, and the right method to repair those broken lives through friendship, work, and happiness.

It is amazing what profound ignorance prevails even among fairly well-informed persons regarding the blind and their feelings, desires, and capabilities. The seeing are apt to conclude that the world of the blind—and especially the deaf-blind person—is quite unlike the sunlit, blooming world they know, that a handicapped person's feelings and sensations are essentially different from their own, and that mental consciousness is fundamentally affected by infirmity. Sighted people blunder still further and imagine that the blind are shut out from all beauty of color, music, and shape. They need to be told over and over that the elements of beauty, order, form, and proportion are tangible to the blind, and that beauty and rhythm are the result of a spiritual law deeper than sense. Yet how many people with eyes take this truth to heart? How many of them take the trouble to ascertain for themselves the fact that the deaf-blind inherit their brain from a seeing and hearing race fitted for five senses and that the spirit fills the silent darkness with its own sunshine and harmony?

Swedenborg had a multitude of similar difficulties in conveying his impressions as a seer to the matter-clogged, mirage-filled senses of his generation. Who knows—perhaps the limitations of the blind who have eyes and the deaf who have ears may yet be a means of carrying God's messages down into the darkest places of man's ignorance and insensibility. Without wishing to be the least bit presumptuous, I hope I may have some skill to use my experience of life in the dark, as Swedenborg used his experience of the spiritual world so that he might elucidate the hidden meanings of the Old and New Testaments. It is a special happiness to me to employ the potency of God's love and its offspring, human love, which stand between me and utter isolation, and to make my misfortunes a medium of help and goodwill to others.

LOVE IS THE INMOST ESSENCE OF MAN

It is an ever-new sorrow to me to realize the tragedy of Swedenborg's opening words in *Divine Love and Wisdom*:

> Man knows that there is such a thing as love; but he
> does not know what love is. . . . And because one is
> unable, when he reflects upon it, to form to himself any
> idea of thought about it, he says either that it is not any-
> thing, or that it is merely something flowing in from
> sight, hearing, touch, or communication with others,
> and thus affecting him. He is wholly unaware that love
> is his very life; not only the general life of his whole
> body and common life of all his thoughts, but also the
> life of all their particulars.

The trouble is, people mistake the utterances, smiles, glances, and gentle deeds of love for love itself. It is just as if I should make the mistake of supposing that the brain thinks from its own power, or the body acts of its own accord, or the voice and tongue cause their own vibrations, or my hand recognizes anything independently of me, when really all these parts of the body are acted upon by the will and mind. Or as if I might place my hand on a beautiful lily and inhale its fragrance and insist that the senses of touch and smell were in the flower when in reality the skin by which I feel produces these sensations. Those are the kinds of appearances that should be guarded against when love, life, and mental activities are discussed.

The common idea of love is that it is something outside of us—a vague sentiment—one of the abstractions that cannot be talked about, because it cannot be distinctly thought about. But Swedenborg teaches that love is not an abstraction without cause, subject, or form. It does not float through the soul or come into being at the touch or sight of an object. It is our inmost essence out of which our spiritual organism is formed, and what we perceive as love is only a sign of that substance. Love actually keeps our faculties alive, as the atmosphere gives the senses of touch, smell, taste, sight, and hearing their sentient life.

I may illustrate the distinction between love and its tokens, for which it is so often mistaken. For unless we have a vivid sense of love's reality, we cannot reach it and change or deepen or purify it so that our affections may be higher, and our joy increased. So often we simply go through the motions of love. We go round and round it in a vicious circle trying to change our tendencies and reconstruct ourselves and others, while love weeps at being left out—or if it be evil, it scoffs at us and hugs itself complacently.

From my own struggle with imperfect speech, I have this example of a wrong, roundabout, indirect method of making over what is marred. It would be absurd to attempt to improve my voice by operating on the sounds it emits as they float through the air. No, I must practice on my vocal organs, and that is of no use either until I improve my inner, or mental, concepts of speech. Voice is not essentially physical; it is thought making itself audible. It is literally shaped, tinted, and modulated by the mind. My supreme effort in practicing is to get true images of sounds and words into my internal ear, since my bodily ear is closed, and the nearer I approach the right use of mind as a speech instrument the better I shall be understood by others.

This seems a far cry from voice to love; but the principle is exactly the same. Our life—with all its emotions, likes, dislikes, and interests—flows, is molded, and colored, and ultimately its vicissitudes are controlled by our inmost love. Therefore, we should strive to realize the true mental concept of love as an active, creating, and dictating power if we wish to acquire nobler feelings, finer ideals, and satisfy our pathetic yearning for happiness.

Love should not be viewed as a detached effect of the soul, or an organ, or a faculty, or a function. Love involves the whole body of conscious thought—intention, purpose, endeavor, motives, and impulses—often suppressed, but always latent, ready at any moment to embody itself in act. It takes on face, hands, and feet through the faculties and organs; it works and talks, and will not be checked by any external circumstance once it begins to move toward an objective. Love, the all-important doctrine, is not a vague, aimless emotion, but the desire for good united with wisdom and fulfilled in right action.

SERVICE: LOVE MADE VISIBLE

Two thousand years ago Jesus clothed himself in flesh that he might walk with men and show them how to live together in peace. Through poverty, through persecution, through betrayal, he lived his life before their eyes, going about his Father's business, healing the sick, comforting the sorrowful, opening the eyes of the blind, and setting free captive minds. He dwelt among the poor and despised, and he ministered to their physical needs.

He told his disciples to go out into the world and to preach the Gospel of Service. He said that the world would not welcome them but this was not to trouble them. They were to be calm and to speak boldly. If a man took their cloaks, they were to give him their coats also, just to show that material things are of secondary importance. Even if people used violence against them, they were warned not to be violent in turn. "They who live by the sword shall perish by the sword," he told them (Matthew 26:52). Love is the power that saves. "Love ye one another as I have loved you, and ye shall be blessed of your Father which is in heaven" (John 13:33; 15:21).

Swedenborg says that "the perfection of man is the love of use," or service to others (*Divine Love and Wisdom*, paragraph 237). Our halting attempts to act are mere stammering suggestions of the greatness of service that we intend. We will to do more than we can ever do, and it is what we will that is in essence ourselves. The dearest of all consolations that Swedenborg's message brings me is that in the next world our narrow field of work shall grow limitlessly broad and luminous. His teachings are full of stimulating faith, of confidence in what he declares he has seen, has heard, and has touched. We who are blind are often glad that another's eye finds a road for us in a wide, perplexing darkness. How much more should we rejoice when a man of vision discovers a way to the radiant outer-lands of the spirit? To our conception of God, the Word, and the hereafter, Swedenborg gives a new actuality that is as startling and as thrilling as the angel-sung tidings of the birth in Bethlehem. He brings fresh testimony to support our hope that the veil will be drawn from our unseeing eyes, that the dull ear will be quickened, and the dumb lips gladdened with speech.

For those who have been stricken blind, Swedenborg's words carry a special message of comfort, for they offer teachings that truly cheer and enlighten. Here and now our misfortune is irreparable. Our service to others is limited. Our thirst for larger activity is unsatisfied. The greatest workers for the race—scientists, poets, and artists who possess all their faculties—are at times shaken with a mighty cry of the soul, a longing more fully to bring forth the energy, the fire, and the richness of imagination and human impulse that overburden them. What wonder, then, that we with our limited senses and more humble powers should crave wider range and scope of usefulness. The difficulties that blindness throws across our paths are grievous. We encounter a thousand restraints, and like all human beings, we seem at times to be accidents and whims of fate. The thwarting of our deep-rooted instincts makes us feel with special poignancy the limitations that beset humanity. If the seeing need hearty, living faith to meet their responsibilities and their trials, imagine how much more the sightless need it.

The blind have a strong friend in Swedenborg's teachings, for they encourage our power to work, to overcome difficulties, and to live the life of the spirit. Swedenborg teaches us that love makes us free, and I can bear witness to its power of lifting us out of the isolation to which we seem condemned. When the idea of an active, all-controlling love lays hold of us, we become masters, creators of good, helpers of our kind. It is as if the dark had sent forth a star to draw us to heaven. We discover in ourselves many undeveloped resources of will and thought. Checked, hampered, failing again and again, we rise above the barriers that bind and confine us; our lives put on serenity and order. In love we find our release from the evils of physical and mental blindness. Our lack of sight forbids our hands to engage in many of the noblest human arts, but love is open to us; and as Swedenborg shows, love teaches us the highest of all arts— the art of living. From his writings we learn how to foster, direct, and practice this restoring love, this constructive, fertile faith, which is the yearning of humanity toward God. For a life in the dark, love is the surest guide.

In our service to others our love is made visible. In service we hear the voice of love and faith that shall at last pronounce the word of eternal life, "Well done!" (Matthew 25:21).

THE DAWNING OF CHRISTIANITY: THE SUN OF LOVE

A young person says, "The acquiescent, conciliatory attitude of the Christian Church toward a corrupt, cruel, and acquisitive society is a repudiation of the Christ Gospel." That statement is indicative of the feeling of many thoughtful people that Christianity is receding rather than growing in power. Some churches realize that their people are leaving them; and, without understanding the cause, they try all manner of expedients to hold their flocks together. They say, "We are living in a materialistic age; we must give the people material attractions in the churches." As a result, we see preacher-actors, concerts, movies, bands, and frenzied acrobatics in some churches. Still, the exodus continues, the people murmur, and the light of faith grows dimmer in their hearts.

What is the cause of this ever-increasing darkness in the tabernacles of God? Why are so many losing their belief in the livability of Christianity? While seeking the answers to these questions, I opened Swedenborg's *True Christian Religion,* and there I found an answer: "Where there is no good of life there is no longer a church." Where people cease to apply their beliefs to practical living there is no faith (cf. chapter VI, "Faith"). Is that not what has happened to the Christian church? No church can inspire noble ideals in the people if it does not follow the aims laid down for us by the Lord.

But the time is coming when society will be so completely transformed that in no way at all will the new order resemble the old. True Christianity will yet inundate the world like the ocean at floodtide; it will overwhelm, submerge, and regenerate mankind. No manufactured barrier of warships, armies, or fortifications will stay the oncoming of these mighty waters. Gender, race, and creed will be washed and purified in the tidal waves of fraternal transformation.

When that day dawns, we will walk with the Sun of Love before our faces, and it will shine whenever two of us look at each other. For the Sun of Love is the substance and the life of all created things. In its bosom lies the future of all things. It is from the Sun of Love that wisdom springs, and through its potency we develop that part of our nature that is patterned after the Divine.

The joy of surmounting obstacles that once seemed
unremovable . . . what other joy is there like it?

GOSPEL OF JOY
In thy presence there is fullness of joy. (Psalm 16:11)

JOY: GOD'S FEAST FOR THE SOUL

Swedenborg's sayings about delight and happiness seem as numberless as the flowers and leaves of a fruit tree in full bloom; and that is not surprising when he declares that the essence of life is in the delight of those things we love. There is no interest when the heart is cold, and where there is no impulse, there is no delight. Human happiness is composed of countless small joys, just as time is made up of minutes and seconds; but few people with all their senses stop to think of this, and still fewer sit down to count their blessings. If they did, they would be kept so busy that the next harsh call to duty would seem like music to their enchanted ears.

I do not refer to hedonism, which is the seeking of pleasure as an end, rather than usefulness. So I hope my words will not seem light to any earnest person when I speak of the universe as a table spread by divine beneficence with a feast for the soul. Every faculty of the mind and every appetite of the body have their own delights, which are the means of renewal and upbuilding. Every single power in human nature, physical and mental, should have a chance to choose and appropriate to itself what is congenial and satisfying.

It is not necessary, as is very often supposed, to give up natural pleasures before we can gain spiritual ones. On the contrary, we enjoy them more exquisitely as we rise in the inner life. How wonderful is a bunch of grapes sent by a dear friend, with its rounded beauty and color and delicious fragrance—love, imagination, and poetry in substance! How rich and varied we find flowers in fragrant delights that quicken the brain and open our heart-blossoms! How endlessly the changes of sky and water and earth charm us and keep before us a lovely mirror of the higher world upon which our faith and our dreams are centered!

The world is so full of care and sorrow that it is a gracious debt we owe to one another to discover the bright crystals of delight hidden in somber circumstances and irksome tasks. Swedenborg, whose labors were like a giant's, saw inexhaustible stores of joy in the midst of exacting routine. Out of his heart and out of heaven's heart he wrote in *True Christian Religion*:

> The joys of love, which are also the joys of charity, cause what is good to be called good; and the charms of wisdom, which are also the charms of faith, cause what is true to be called true; for joys and charms of various kinds make their life, and without life from these, goods and truths are like inanimate things, and are also unfruitful. (paragraph 38)

As selfishness and complaint pervert and cloud the mind, so love with its joy clears and sharpens the vision. Love provides the delicacy of perception to see wonders in what before seemed dull and trivial. It replenishes the springs of inspiration, and its joy sends a river of new life flowing like blood through matter-clogged faculties.

EDUCATION BY DELIGHT

There is a growing sentiment among thoughtful people that delight is essential to growth and self-improvement and the acquisition of nobler instincts. What induces children to learn but their delight in knowing? Do not the pleasures of taste enable the body to assimilate food? What mind that thinks at all does not choose the ideas that please it and let all others go unheeded? What else do we do with our secret inner will except focus it upon some El Dorado that allures us and bid us to follow until we can realize our dreams? What other than dreaming of delight leads on the brave and adventurous to fresh discoveries and the increase of humanity's natural resources? Why does the scientist often endure mental travail and repulsive tasks, if not for the delight felt in understanding new truths or rendering a new service to others?

A wise teacher or friend or true reformer does not attempt to drag a wrongdoer into the right way by force. Skillfully combining discipline with pleasant influences, the teacher works to soften the stubborn will and charm the sullen mind into right thinking. Anyone who, out of sheer goodness of heart, speaks a helpful word, gives a cheering smile, or smooths over a rough place in another's path knows that the delight felt in the giving is so returned as to make it an intimate part of one's own life— a rule to live by. The joy of surmounting obstacles that once seemed unremovable and pushing the frontier of accomplishment further—what other joy is there like it? If those who seek happiness would only stop one little minute and think, they would see that the delights they really experience are as countless as the blades of grass at their feet or the drops of dew sparkling upon the morning flowers.

Yet how few persons I meet realize this wealth of joy! It is a marvel and a sorrow to me to observe how far afield they go in pursuit of happiness. They look for it in the strangest of places. They visit kings and queens and bow to them; they seek happiness in travel and excitement; they dig for it in the depths of the earth, thinking that it lies in hidden treasure. Many others rob themselves of joy by superstitiously fettering their intellect for the sake of religion or convention or party policy. They are blinded, deafened, and starved when all the time there is within them a world of sweet wealth ready to bless their hearts and minds. It is God's good gift to them out of his happiness, and they do not even know it.

OUR JOY GIVES US STRENGTH

To help people find themselves is often to surprise them with new-found joy. For delight serves as a means of self-knowledge. Swedenborg says if people examine their personal delights, they will often realize they are self-centered because most of their energies are directed to shaping their own lives or acquiring knowledge for private ends; but it turns out that the more enduring joys are born of an unselfish purpose to serve others and create new life in the world. These selfless delights will whisper approval to all and urge them to rise above their self-centeredness into a consciousness of new powers and new self-insights. Only when people trace the footsteps of their spirit to the home of its delights will they behold their own form and face and read their fate in the book of life.

But Swedenborg also says that if people with unlovely delights have the intellectual honesty to acknowledge them, and earnestly try to lift up their hearts to something worthy, there will be no reason for despair. As fast as old fascinations depart, pure happiness will rush into the soul as irresistibly as strong air currents that gladden a long shut-up dwelling; and the happier people become, the greater will be their strength to change outward circumstances to their own desire. It is a mistake for people to entertain fears about enemies finding a breach in their once-broken ramparts. In place of each fear, they can build a new delight and concentrate on it until the ordeal passes.

That is what is meant by "recreation," and it is wonderful to read how many unfortunate men and women are being thus helped out of seemingly hopeless evil tendencies into undreamed self-development, a heaven-given psychotherapy. Forgiveness for sin is nothing but the well-spring of joy from above that fills the bruised heart when one has driven out wrong desires and evil thoughts, and works in harmony with the powers of good.

It is beyond a doubt that everyone should have time for a hobby or some special delight, if only five minutes each day to seek out a lovely flower or cloud or a star, or learn a verse or brighten another's dull task. What is the use of such terrible diligence as many tire themselves out with, always postponing the experience of beauty and joy while they cling to irksome duties? Until they admit these fair, fresh, and eternal presences into their lives, they shut themselves out of heaven, and a gray dust settles on all their existence. That the sky is brighter than the earth means little unless the earth itself is appreciated and enjoyed. Loving what is of this earth gives the right to aspire to the radiance of the sunrise and the stars.

Few people are saints or geniuses; but there is always this hope for all of us—that every pure delight we cherish is a focus of good-will, and every lovely scene we dwell on, every harmony we listen to, every graceful or tender thing touched with reverent hands inspires a flock of sweet thoughts that neither care nor poverty nor pain can destroy.

Joy is inseparable from the doctrines set forth by Swedenborg. In that day, his was a new branch of philosophy that seemed strange after the penances of the Middle Ages and the gloom of iron creeds. One of the surprises of his teaching is the concept of delight as a minister to life. His superb faith in the human ability to discover the deeper joys of marriage and to augment the happiness of childhood is still far ahead of the timid distrust, the low ideals, and the stupid methods of imparting knowledge that prevail among us. In Swedenborg's philosophy, true life is the heart's capacity for joy fulfilled.

OVERCOMING

Be of good cheer, I have overcome the world. (John 16:33)

WE ARE HERE FOR A PURPOSE

Once affliction was looked upon as a punishment from God—a burden to be borne passively and piously. People believed that the only way to help victims of misfortune was to shelter them and leave them to meditate and live as contentedly as possible in the valley of the shadow. But now we understand that a sequestered life without aspiration enfeebles the spirit.

It is exactly the same as with the body. The muscles must be used, or they lose their strength. If we do not go out of our limited experience somehow and use our memory, understanding, and sympathy, they become inactive. It is by fighting the limitations, temptations, and failures of the world that we reach our highest possibilities. That is what Swedenborg calls renouncing the world and worshiping God.

Sick or well, blind or seeing, bound or free, we are here for a purpose, and however we are situated, we please God better with useful deeds than with many prayers or pious resignation. The temple or church is empty unless the good of life fills it. It is not the stone walls that make it small or large, but the brave souls' light shining around and in it. The altar is holy only when it represents the altar of our heart upon which we offer the only sacrifices ever commanded—the love that is stronger than hate and the faith that overcomes doubt.

REFINEMENT OF THE SOUL

A simple, childlike faith in a Divine Friend solves all the problems that come to us upon this earth. Difficulties meet us at every turn. They are an accompaniment of life that results from the combination of character and individual idiosyncracies. The surest way to meet them is to assume that we are immortal and that we have a Friend who "slumbers not, nor sleeps" (Psalm. 121:4), and who watches over us and guides us—if we but let him.

I have never believed that my limitations were in any sense punishments or accidents. If I had held such a view, I could never have exerted the strength to overcome them. I thank God for my handicaps; for through them, I have found myself, my work, and my God. It has always seemed to me that there is a very special significance to the words of the Epistle to the Hebrews: "If we are chastened, God dealeth with us as with sons" (Hebrews 12:6). Swedenborg's teachings confirm this view. He defines the greatly misunderstood word *chastening* or *chastisement*, not as punishment, but as training, discipline, and refinement of the soul. With this thought strongly entrenched in our innermost being, we can do almost anything we wish and need not limit the things we think. We may help ourselves to all the beauty of the universe that we can hold.

For every hurt there is recompense of tender sympathy. Out of pain grow the violets of patience and sweetness, the vision of the holy fire that touched the lips of Isaiah and kindled his life into spirit, and the contentment that comes with the evening star. The marvelous richness of human experience would lose something of rewarding joy if there were no limitations to overcome. The hilltop hour would not be half so wonderful if there were no dark valley to traverse.

Swedenborg's *True Christian Religion* is full of stimuli for faith in our God-given powers and self-activity. The chapters "Faith" and "Free Will" are a powerful declaration that we should never surrender to misfortune or circumstances or even to our faults hopelessly or passively—as if we were but carved images with our hands hanging down, waiting for God's grace to put us into motion. We should not succumb to spiritual slavery. We should take the initiative, look into ourselves fearlessly, and search out new ideas of what to do and ways to develop our will-power. Then God will give us enough light and love for all our needs.

Now, limitations of all kinds are forms of chastening to encourage self-development and true freedom. They are tools put into our hands to hew away the stone and flint that keep hidden our higher gifts. They tear away the blindfold of indifference from our eyes, and we behold the burdens others are carrying, learning to help them by yielding to the compassionate dictates of our hearts.

OPENING THE INNER EYE

The example of newly blinded people is so concrete I wish to use it as a type for all life training. When they first lose sight, they may think there is nothing left but heartache and despair. They feel shut out from all that is human. Life is like ashes on a cold hearth. The fire of ambition is quenched. The light of hope is gone. Objects once delightful seem to thrust out sharp edges as they grope their way about. Even those who love them act unwittingly as an irritant to their feelings because the blind feel they can no longer give others the support of their labor.

Then comes some wise teacher and friend to assure the handicapped that they can work with their hands and to a considerable degree train hearing to take the place of sight. Often the stricken do not believe it and, in despair, interpret it as mockery. Like those who are drowning, they strike blindly at anyone who tries to help. Nevertheless, the sufferers must be urged onward, and when the realization comes that they can once again connect with the world and fulfill the tasks of humanity, they find unfolding within them a being not dreamed of before. If they are wise, they discover at last that happiness has very little to do with outward circumstances, and they walk the darkened path with a firmer will than they ever felt in the light.

Likewise those who have been mentally blinded "in the gradual furnace of the world" can, and must, be pressed to look for new capabilities within themselves and work out new ways to happiness. They may even resent a faith that expects nobler things from them. They may say in effect, "I will be content if you take me for what I am—dull, or mean, or hard, or selfish." But it is an affront to them and to the eternal dignity of humanity to acquiesce to this request. There is much within us that even our nearest friends cannot know—more than we dare or care or are able to bare to them—more of feeling, more of power, more of character. How little we know ourselves! We need limitations and temptations to open our inner selves, dispel our ignorance, tear off our disguises, throw down old idols, and destroy false standards. Only by such rude awakenings can we be led to a place where we are less cramped, less hindered by the ever-insistent external world. Only then do we discover a new capacity and appreciation of goodness and beauty and truth.

From such experience we may gain a wonderful interpretation of the words of Jesus: "Verily, verily, I say unto you, he that receiveth whomsoever I send receiveth me" (John 13:20). We may know that in every limitation we overcome, and in the higher ideals we thus attain, the whole kingdom of love and wisdom is present. In this way, we learn that the real way to grow is by aspiring beyond our limitations, by wishing sublimely for great things, and by striving to achieve them. Thus we grow increasingly conscious of the deeper meaning of our lives.

The eye grows by learning to see more in particular objects. To our physical sight the earth looks flat, and the stars are the same to us as they were to the ancients. Yet science has opened up infinite new wonders and glories in these phenomena. Children see in the things about them only what they want or do not want, but when a Newton recognizes the falling of the apple as the expression of a universal force in nature, he sees far beyond ordinary sight. It is the same with our spirits. We grow as we discern more fully the possibilities of new life wrapped up in daily contacts. But when we forget or ignore this vital fact, the senses lead us astray. That is why limitations are necessary—to bring before us the greatness of inner life and to show us our God-given opportunities in every moment.

In every limitation we overcome, and in the higher ideals
we thus attain, the whole kingdom of love and wisdom is present.

TAKE YOUR CHOICE

The constant service of Swedenborg lies in thoughts such as these. He shows us that, in every event and every limitation, we have a choice, and that to choose is to create. We can decide to let our trials crush us, or we can convert them to new forces of good. We can drift along with general opinion and tradition, or we can throw ourselves upon the guidance of the soul within and steer courageously toward truth.

We cannot tell from the outside whether our experiences are really blessings or not. They are cups of poison or cups of healthful life, according to what we ourselves put into them. The choices offered us are never so much between what we may or may not do, as between *the principles from which we act* when we are thwarted and limited. Earth is not intended to be an altogether delightful abode any more than it is meant to be a place of wrath. As the soil brings forth thistles and as roses have thorns, human life will have its trials. It is not strange or cruel. It is the urge of God that impels us to enlarge our lives and keep strong for a higher destiny that cannot be accomplished within these earthly limits. Only by striving for what is beyond us will we win expansion and joy. Let us, then, take up those limitations that each of us has and follow the example of he who bore upon his frail human shoulders the cross of the world that he might become a luminous and inspiring influence, communicating life-giving thoughts and desires to the weak, the tempted, and the despondent.

Truly I have looked into the very heart of darkness and refused to yield to its paralyzing influence, but in spirit I am one of those who walk the morning. What if all dark, discouraging moods of the human mind come across my way as thick as the dry leaves of autumn? Other feet have travelled that road before me, and I know the desert leads to God as surely as the green, refreshing fields and fruitful orchards.

I, too, have been profoundly humiliated and brought to realize my smallness amid the immensity of creation. The more I learn, the less I think I know; and the more I understand of my sense-experience, the more I perceive its shortcomings and its inadequacy as a basis of life. Sometimes the points of view of the optimist and the pessimist seem so well-balanced to me that it is only by sheer force of spirit that I can keep my hold upon a practical, livable philosophy of life. But I use my will, choose life, and reject its opposite, nothingness.

Edwin Markham has exquisitely wrought into his poem, "Take Your Choice," the opposing moods and different beliefs that contend for supremacy today:

> On the bough of the rose is the prickling briar;
> The delicate lily must live in the mire;
> The hues of the butterfly go at a breath;
> At the end of the road is the house of death.
>
> Nay, nay: on the briar is the delicate rose;
> In the mire of the river the lily blows;
> The moth is as fair as the flower of the sod;
> At the end of the road is a door to God!

THE MYSTIC SENSE

Behold, the Kingdom of God is within you. (Luke 17:21)

OTHERWORLDLINESS

It is all very well to talk about the folly of "otherworldliness," but men have tried living without it and ended in tragic failure. Sadly, the vast majority of human beings have shut themselves off from their splendid possibilities for inner development, living as though they were trapped and powerless under a dead weight.

Swedenborg, one of those rare individuals who saw the way out, wrote these words: "Truths derived from good have all power" (*Arcana Coelestia*, paragraph 10182:5). Through these words he taught that the strength of Samson would be available to each of us mentally if only we would let God inspire us directly from his Divine Truth.

It is significant that Ralph Waldo Emerson, who stood at a great distance from Swedenborg in many beliefs, saw the fundamental truth behind Swedenborg's selfless attitude and wrote: "The weakness of the will begins when the individual would be something of himself, and the blindness of the intellect begins when it would be something of itself." Both Swedenborg and Emerson understood that nothing but letting the Divine Life have its way through us will deliver the world. This is the true significance of Swedenborg's message from "the hills whence cometh our help" (Psalm 121:1).

It was not immortality or otherworldliness that Swedenborg stressed, but the responsibilities it imposes upon us. He did not regard his extraordinary communication with angels as an end in itself, but only as a means for opening his understanding to a true interpretation of God's Word and of making the knowledge thus acquired the common heritage of mankind. In fact, there is no such thing as "otherworldliness" when we are convinced that heaven is not beyond us but within us. We are only urged so much more to act, to love, to hope against hope, and to resolutely tinge the darkness about us with the beautiful hues of our indwelling heaven, here and now.

It must be understood that, while the possibility of communicating with departed spirits is conceded, we are never encouraged to cultivate it. When prophets, apostles, and seers are needed to wake our sleeping hearts, it is useful for them to be in conscious association with angels and spirits because God then supervises the work himself and prevents confusion. But as a rule, any communication with spirits that we initiate exposes us to great danger, because we are so easily influenced by deceiving spirits who know our weaknesses and use us for selfish purposes.

If, therefore, Swedenborg states that every human being is attended by at least two angels from heaven and two bad spirits from hell, he also maintains that our peace of mind and order-

There is no such thing as "otherworldliness" when we are
convinced that heaven is not beyond us but within us.

liness of life depend upon our being unconscious of our invisible allies and enemies. It is enough for us to follow the Lord alone, trusting to his protection and guidance.

THE SOURCE OF THE MYSTIC SENSE

Possibly my own partial isolation from the world of light and sound gives me insight into Swedenborg's extraordinary experience. I do not know if it is the "mystic" sense I possess; but certainly it is perceptive. It is the faculty that brings distant objects within the cognizance of the blind so that even the stars seem to be at our very door. This sense relates me to the spiritual world. It surveys the limited experience I gain from an imperfect touch-world and presents it to my mind for spiritualization. This sense reveals the Divine to the human in me; it forms a bond between earth and the great beyond, between now and eternity, between God and humanity. It is speculative, intuitive, reminiscent.

There is not only an objective physical world but also an objective spiritual world. The spiritual has an outside as well as an inside, just as the physical has an inside and outside. Each has its own level of reality. There is no antagonism between these two planes of life, except when the material is used without regard to the spiritual that lies within and above it.

The distinction between them is explained by Swedenborg in his theory of discrete degrees. He illustrates this by saying that the physical world is perceived by a sensory apparatus that is of the same substance as the physical world, while the spiritual world is perceived by a sensory apparatus that is of the same substance as that of the spiritual world.

My life is so complicated by a triple handicap of blindness, deafness, and imperfect speech that I cannot do the simplest thing without thought and effort to rationalize my experiences. If I employed this mystic sense constantly without trying to understand the outside world, my progress would be checked, and everything would fall about me in chaos. It is easy for me to mix up dreams and reality, the spiritual and the physical that I have not properly visualized; without discernment I could not keep them apart. So even if I commit errors in forming concepts of color, sound, light, and intangible phenomena, I must always try to preserve equilibrium between my outer and inner life. Neither can I use my sense of touch without reference to the experience of others. Without the help of those who see, I would go astray or else go round and round in a blind circle.

I have always been especially helped by this passage from Swedenborg's *Arcana Coelestia* (paragraph 5119):

> It appears as if the things which are in the world flow in through the senses toward the interiors, but this is a fallacy of sense. The influx is of interiors into exteriors, and by means of this influx man has perception. . . . It is the interior man that sees and perceives what goes on outside of him, and from this interior source the sense-experience has its life; for from no other than this subjective source is there any faculty of feeling or sensation. But the fallacy that the sense comes from the outside is of such a nature and so common that the natural mind cannot rid itself of it, nor even the rational mind, until it can think abstractly apart from the senses.

I can easily believe that, as Swedenborg often tries to show us, the visible and tangible phenomena of the world are the direct embodiments of the mental states of its inhabitants. It is of little use to know about even the most wonderful splendors of heaven unless we understand something of their origin and their essential meaning. Naturally this is difficult for those who do not sense the separateness between their earthly bodies and their inner selves.

PSYCHIC POWER

My life enlarged when, at the age of eleven, I learned to speak. I can never cease to marvel and be excited by that event of thirty-six years ago; it stands out so isolated, miraculous, baffling. Think of transforming mute, soulless air into speech in the midst of midnight silence. Literally, I had no concepts of speech, and my touch did not suffice to convey to me the thousand fine vibrations of spoken words. Without physical hearing, I had to exert the utmost thought of which I was capable until I succeeded in making myself not only heard but understood.

It is only by sheer force of mind even now that I keep my speech anywhere near intelligible. When I speak best, I am at a loss to maintain that degree of perfection because I cannot fully sense the tones going forth from my lips. What surprises me is not that I fail, but that the subconscious part or the spirit enters so often into my clumsy speech, and my friends say earnestly, "Why can you not talk as well as that always?" If I could develop that psychic power more fully, I feel sure that my victory would be complete.

The pain and disappointment I have endured are incalculable; but they are a price worth paying for the joy I have in being able to keep this living bond between the outer world and myself. As I learned to articulate and to put feeling into what I said, I sensed more and more the miracle of all time and eternity—the reality of thought. Thought, out of which are wrought books, philosophies, sciences, civilizations, and indeed the joy and the woe of the human race.

IN THE GREAT SILENCE OF MY THOUGHTS . . .

In the great silence of my thoughts all those whom I have loved on earth, whether near or far, living or dead, live and have their own individuality, their own dear ways and charm. At any moment I can bring them around me to cheer my loneliness. It would break my heart if any barrier could prevent them from coming to me. But I know there are two worlds—one we can measure with line and rule, and the other we can feel with our hearts and intuitions.

My steadfast thought rises above the treason of my eyes to follow sight beyond all temporal seeing. Suppose there are a million chances against that one that my loved ones who have gone are alive. What of it? I will take that one chance and risk mistake, rather than let my doubts sadden their souls and find out afterward. Since there is that one chance of immortality, I will endeavor not to cast a shadow upon the joy of the departed. I sometimes wonder who needs cheer more, the one who gropes on here below or the one who is perhaps just learning truly to see in God's light.

How real is the darkness to one who only guesses in the shadows of earth at an unseen sun! But how well worth the effort it is to keep spiritually in touch with those who have loved us to their last moment upon earth! Certainly it is one of our sweetest experiences that when we are touched by some noble affection or pure joy, we remember the dead most tenderly and feel powerfully drawn to them. And always the consciousness of such a faith has the power to change the face of mortality, make adversity a winning fight, and set up a beacon of encouragement for those whose last support of joy seems taken from them.

COMMUNION WITH GOD

I have read with emotion the words of the brilliant English chemist Sir Humphry Davy, in whom science, faith, and unselfishness were combined to a remarkable degree:

> I envy no quality of mind or intellect in others—not genius, power, wit, or fancy; but if I could choose what would be most delightful, and I believe most useful to me, I should prefer a firm religious belief to any other blessing; for it makes life a discipline of goodness, creates new hopes when all earthly hopes vanish, . . . awakens life even in death, and from corruption and decay calls up beauty and divinity; makes an instrument of torture and shame [the cross] the ladder of ascent to Paradise; and far above all combinations of earthly hopes, calls up the most delightful visions of palms and amaranths, the gardens of the blest, the security of everlasting joys, where the sensualist and the skeptic view only gloom, decay, annihilation, and despair.

It is like a Pentecostal experience to touch these words and feel in my hand the strong hand of a calm and scientific man and a lover of mankind, who had no reconciler to second his thought, who saw the countless contradictions of the old faiths, who knew the tortures of natural existence, but who kept unshaken his communion with his God.

I cannot imagine myself living without religion. I could as easily fancy a living body without a heart. To one who is deaf and blind, the spiritual world offers no difficulty. Nearly everything in the natural world is as vague, as remote from my senses, as spiritual things seem to the minds of most people. But the inner or mystic sense, if you like, gives me vision of the unseen.

I am aware that some learned critics will break me on the wheel of their disdain. They will try to mend my poor philosophy on the anvil of their keen mirth with the hammer of reasons culled from science. They say that "all creation crowns itself in this invisible atom of matter. It is the beginning and the end." Perhaps; but there is still a dewdrop in the lily's cup; there is a fragrance in the heart of the rose, and under a leaf a bird folds its wings!

My mystic world is lovely with trees and clouds and stars and eddying streams I have never "seen." I am often conscious of beautiful flowers and birds and laughing children where to my seeing associates there is nothing. They skeptically declare that I see "light that never was on sea or land." But I know that their mystic sense is dormant, and that is why there are so many barren places in their lives. They prefer "facts" to vision. They want a scientific demonstration, and they can have it. Science with untiring patience traces mankind back to the ape and rests content. It is out of this ape that God creates the seer, and science meets spirit as life meets death. With steadfast thought I follow sight beyond all seeing, until my soul stands up in spiritual light and cries, "Life and death are one!"

CREDO

What is so sweet as to wake from a troubled dream and behold a beloved face smiling upon you? I love to believe that such shall be our awakening from earth to heaven.

I believe in the immortality of the soul because I have within me immortal longings. I believe that the state we enter after death is wrought of our own motives, thoughts, and deeds. I believe that when the eyes within my physical eyes open upon the world to come, I will be consciously living in the country of my heart. Without this faith there would be little meaning in my life.

My faith never wavers that each dear friend I have "lost" is a link between this world and the next. My spirit is, for the moment, bowed down with grief when I cease to feel the touch of their hands or hear a tender word from them; but the light of faith never fades from my sky, and I take heart again, glad that they are free.

I cannot understand the poor faith that fears to look into the eyes of death. Faith that is vulnerable in the presence of death is a frail reed to lean upon. Life here is more cruel than death. Life divides and estranges, while death, which at heart is life eternal, reunites and reconciles. When I review my life, it seems to me that my most precious obligations are to those whom I have never seen. My dearest intimacies are those of the mind; my most loyal and helpful friends are those of the spirit.

As I wander through the dark, encountering difficulties, I am aware of encouraging voices that murmur from the spirit realm. I sense a holy passion pouring down from the springs of infinity. I thrill to music that beats with the pulses of God. Bound to suns and planets by invisible cords, I feel the flame of eternity in my soul. Here, in the midst of everyday air, I sense the rush of ethereal rains. I am conscious of the splendor that binds all things of the earth to all things of heaven. Immured by silence and darkness, I possess the light that will give me vision a thousandfold—when death sets me free.

It was his mission to teach people to listen to the inward voice
rather than to opinions and disputations.

THE GREAT MESSAGE

The Lord my God will enlighten my darkness.
(Psalm 18:28)

LOVE AS A TORCH

Many years have passed since Swedenborg's death, and slowly his achievements have been winning recognition. The antagonism that his doctrines once aroused has changed to an attitude of tolerance and inquiry. Many intelligent people have advocated his teachings in the centers of civilization and carried them to nooks and corners of the world undreamed of by most of us. His message has traveled like light, side by side with new science, the new freedom, and the new society, which are struggling to realize themselves in the life of humanity.

I keep coming across instances of handicapped or disappointed lives that have been enriched and brightened by that Great Message. I, too, have my humble testimony, and I shall be most happy if through a word of mine even one individual gains a sweeter sense of God's presence or a keener zest for mastering the difficulties of outward environment.

For of one thing I am sure: any effort is worthwhile that brings comfort to limited, struggling human beings in a dark, self-centered age. There is still among us a distressing indifference to all things of faith and an impatience at any effort to explain the laws of life in spiritual terms. The only really blind are those who will not see the truth—those who shut their eyes to spiritual vision. For them alone darkness is irrevocable.

Those who explore the dark with love as a torch and trust as a guide find it good. Blind people who have inner vision know that they live in a spiritual world inconceivably more wonderful than the material world that is veiled from them. The landscapes they behold never fade. The flowers they look upon are the immortal flowers that grow in God's garden. For such people, Swedenborg's message is like the rock smitten by Moses, yielding sweet streams of healing water, even an abundance of truths for those who hunger and thirst in their pilgrimage through an age of materialism and selfishness.

RELIGION IN LIFE

While the theological teachings of Swedenborg are in many long volumes, his central doctrine is simple. It consists of three main ideas: God as Divine Love, God as Divine Wisdom, and God as Divine Power for use. These ideas come as waves from an ocean that floods every bay and harbor of life with new potency of will, of faith, and of effort. The conclusion forces itself upon the mind of one who diligently reads his works, that Swedenborg described a world that was as distinctly objective to him as the world we live in is to us.

Swedenborg shows that the physical world presents a system of perfect order, and every part of it fits into every other part. He shows that these same laws apply to the constitution of the spiritual realm, the interpretation of the Bible, and the mind of man. The reader who believes in revelation will find convincing evidence of Swedenborg's teachings in the Bible itself.

Three characteristics of his philosophy are completeness, homogeneity, and the universal adaptability of its principles. As a leaf grows out of a twig, or as the body depends on the mind, so is any part of this system bound to any related part. All through his theological works, Swedenborg shows that all true religion is of the life and that the life of religion is to do good. He also tells us that the Word—the law of life—has its fullness, its holiness, and its power, in the sense of the letter and in our acts. Every parable, every spiritual truth in the Bible, demands our faithful performance of every service essential to the health, enlightenment, and liberation of humankind. This means that we must strive to fill the practicalities of the world with the spirit. For heaven, as Swedenborg depicts it, is not a mere collection of radiant ideas but a practical, livable world.

OUR SACRED RESPONSIBILITY

Swedenborg's claims have indeed astonished the world ever since they were made. He said,

> It is not unknown to me that many will say that a man can never speak with spirits and angels while he lives in the body; and many that it is fantasy, others that I state such things to gain credit, others other things; but I do

not hesitate on this account, for I have seen, I have heard, I have felt. (*Arcana Coelestia*, paragraph 68)

I have read with wonderment that students of psychic life, such as Sir Oliver Lodge, have scarcely referred to Swedenborg's voluminous works dealing with the same subject. Lodge published a number of interviews with his "dead" son, Raymond, who told how the inhabitants of eternity do the work they like best and live in the company they like best, how they are fed and clothed. But the information thus conveyed is scanty and fragmentary. It was extracted by elaborate rappings, and in a manner not at all resembling Swedenborg's face-to-face conversations with angels and spirits, or his superhuman poise while he noted a multitude of rational happenings and visible truths sparkling like diamonds. Swedenborg saw memory ossified; he heard the complaints of bad spirits when they looked into heaven and saw thick darkness. He found that angels could not breathe in an atmosphere to which their thoughts had not raised them, and he saw the delicious fruits of charity that nourish both body and mind.

When we think of all those who would rejoice to have colorful details of that unseen world to which their loved ones have gone, the sacred responsibility of satisfying their doubting hearts is obvious. They can rejoice to know that in the eighteenth century there arose a trained scientist who found himself a seer and gave to the world without any profit for himself twenty-five, stout quarto volumes crammed full of details of definite contacts with the spiritual universe. He stood right up to his claim, let his wealth go, lived simply, printed all his own works, and distributed them in a humble yet dignified manner. He remained cool in temperament, weighing all he did and said. He never showed signs of being racked by passion or impulse or any excitement of a supernatural kind. He never forsook his inductive habits of thinking or denied any physical reality or scorned the smallest joys of his fellow men. No matter how absorbed he was in his staggering mission, he responded to every demand for his assistance or sympathy in the practical needs of daily life.

On his deathbed, he was asked if all he had written was strictly true or if he wished any parts to be retracted, and he replied with unfaltering warmth:

> I have written nothing but the truth, as you will have it more and more confirmed hereafter all the days of your life, provided you always keep close to the Lord, and faithfully serve Him alone, in shunning evils of all kinds as sins against Him, and diligently searching His Sacred Word, which from beginning to end bears incontestable testimony to the truth of the doctrines I have delivered to the world. (Tafel 1877, II: 580)

HOW I WOULD HELP THE WORLD

Since I was sixteen years old, I have been a strong believer in the doctrines given to the world by Emanuel Swedenborg. It was his mission to teach people to listen to the inward voice rather than to opinions and disputations. After many years of reverent study of the Bible, I gratefully wonder if I am not more indebted to Swedenborg for the faith that turns my darkness into light than I have yet realized. I acknowledge my profound indebtedness to Swedenborg for a richer interpretation of the Bible, a deeper understanding of the meaning of Christianity, and a precious sense of the Divine Presence in the world.

The doctrines set forth by Swedenborg bring us by a wondrous path to God's City of Light. I have walked through its sunlit ways of truth; I have drunk of its sweet waters of knowledge; and the eyes of my spirit have been opened, so that I know the joy of vision that conquers darkness and circles heaven.

Swedenborg's message has meant so much to me! It has given color and reality and unity to my thought of the life to come; it has exalted my ideas of love, truth, and usefulness; it has been my strongest incitement to overcome limitations.

There is an exquisitely quieting and soothing power in the thoughts of Swedenborg for people of my temperament. His *Divine Love and Wisdom* is a fountain of life that I am always happy to be near. I find in it a happy rest from the noisy insanity of the outer world with its many words of little meaning and actions of little worth. I bury my fingers in this great river of light that is higher than all the stars, deeper than the silence that enfolds me. It alone is great, while all else is small, fragmentary.

The atmosphere Swedenborg creates absorbs me completely. His slightest phrase is significant to me. I plunge my hands deep into my large Braille volumes containing Swedenborg's teachings, and withdraw them full of the secrets of the spiritual world. I wish I might be able to radiate the spiritual illumination that came to me when I read with my own fingers *Heaven and Hell*. All the days of my life have since "proved the doctrine" and found it true.

Were I but capable of interpreting to others one-half of the stimulating thoughts and noble sentiments that are buried in Swedenborg's writings, I should help them more than I am ever likely to in any other way. It would be such a joy to me if I might be the instrument of bringing Swedenborg to a world that is spiritually deaf and blind. His volumes are an inexhaustible well-spring of satisfaction to those who lead the life of the mind. If people would only begin to read Swedenborg's books with at first a little patience, they would soon be reading them for pure joy.

Immured by silence and darkness, I possess the light that will give me vision a thousandfold—when death sets me free.

MY LUMINOUS UNIVERSE

And I saw a new heaven and a new earth.
(Revelation 21:1)

IT IS DIFFICULT FOR ME TO ANSWER WHEN I AM ASKED WHAT are the main lessons life has taught me. Looking deeply into my inner self, I feel that ultimately I have not been influenced by any particular "lessons," but by forces working on my subconscious that have borne me on an unseen current.

Instinctively, I found my greatest satisfaction in working with men and women everywhere who ask not, "Shall I labor among Christians or Jews or Buddhists?" but say rather, "God, in thy wisdom help me to decrease the sorrows of thy children and increase their advantages and joys." Blindness and deafness were simply the banks that guided the course of my life-ship until the stream joined the sea.

I have caught rays of light from different thinkers—Socrates, Plato, Bacon, Kant, and Emanuel Swedenborg, the Swedish mystic. With Socrates, I believe in thinking out the meaning of words before committing them to speech. Plato's theory of the Absolute strengthens me because it gives truth to what I know is true, beauty to the beautiful, music to what I cannot hear, and light to what I cannot see. Swedenborg has shaken down the barriers of time and space in my life and supplied me with likenesses or correspondences between the world within and the world without, which give me courage and imagination beyond my three senses.

Thus I move from one philosophy to another, constructing out of a fragmentary outward environment a luminous, resonant universe.

These varied thoughts convince me that, blind or seeing, one is not happy unless one's heart is filled with the sun that never dissolves into gloom. God is that sun, and if one's faith in him is only strong, he will somehow or other reveal one's powers and brighten the darkest days with his divine beams.

Since my seventeenth year, I have tried to live according to the teachings of Emanuel Swedenborg. By "church," he did not mean an ecclesiastical organization, but a spiritual fellowship of thoughtful men and women who spend their lives in a service to mankind that outlasts them. He called it a civilization that was to be born of a healthy, universal religion—goodwill, mutual understanding, service from each to all, regardless of dogma or ritual.

Swedenborg's religious works are in many long volumes, but their sum and substance are in three main ideas—God as Divine Love, God as Divine Wisdom, and God as Divine Power for use.

By love, I do not mean a vague, aimless sentiment, but a desire for good united with wisdom and fulfilled in work and deed. Because God is infinite, he puts resources into each human being that outrun the possibilities of evil. He is always creating in us new forms of self-development and channels through which, even if unaware, we may quicken new impulses toward civilization, art, or humanitarianism.

My confidence in the final triumph of idealism over materialism does not spring from closing my mental eyes to the suffering or the evildoing of men, but rather from a steadfast belief that goodwill climbs upward in human nature while meanness and hatred drop into their native nothingness, and life goes on with unabated vigor to its new earth and heaven.

With me, optimism has changed from the hard bud of girlhood to a fuller knowledge of human affairs and the tragedies and horrors that often seem to pervert men from God's Plan of Good. But my faith in progress has not wavered.

In my travels around the world, I have witnessed here and there wonderful awakenings to spiritual truth and a sense of responsibility for the welfare of the blind, the deaf, and other unfortunate beings, which would be impossible if there were not a growing desire for the common good of mankind.

I believe that we begin heaven now and here if we do our work for others faithfully. There is no useful work that is not part of the welfare of mankind. Even the humblest occupation is "skilled labor" if it contains an effort above mere self-support to serve a spiritual or social need.

I have a joyous sense of personal immortality. Life in the other world is just as real and full of change and wonder as on earth, but one is given eyes and ears to perceive far more clearly the varieties of good and constructive thought that the flesh conceals on earth.

As I look to the future, I feel the thrill of challenge to greater self-realization. I do not know what I shall do in the coming years, but I shall continue whatever services I can to the blind and others who are handicapped. I want to survey quietly the treasures of thought that I have gathered, but have not had the leisure to explore.

There are two ways to look at destiny, one from below and the other from above. In one view, we are being pushed by irresistible forces, obsessed by the fear that war, ignorance, and poverty will never be abolished. But looking up to the clock of Truth, I see that man has been civilized only a few minutes, and I rest in the assurance that, out of the problems that disturb thinking minds and warm hearts, there shall break the morning star of universal peace.

EPILOGUE: THE VOICE IN MY SILENCE

Ray Silverman, editor and reviser

Be faithful unto death. And I will give you
the crown of life. (Revelation 2:10)

"GO AND TEACH . . ."

THE BOOK YOU HAVE JUST FINISHED READING IS A REVISION of Helen Keller's tribute to Emanuel Swedenborg. It was written in 1927 and titled *My Religion*. In that book, Helen referred to Swedenborg as "the light-bringer of my blindness" and said that his message had been "my strongest incitement to overcome limitations."

Beginning in 1893, at the age of thirteen when she first met John Hitz, and then again at the age of sixteen when Hitz gave her one of Swedenborg's books, Helen gradually embraced the teachings of the New Church. "As I grew to womanhood," she said, "I took more and more to the teachings of the New Church as my religion." According to Helen's own testimony, Swedenborg's message had satisfied the inmost longings and highest aspirations of her spirit. "I am a Swedenborgian," she said. "Its spirituality and idealism appeal to me. It also fosters all kinds of true freedom, places humanity above party, country, race, and it never loses sight of the essence of Jesus's gospel—the supreme and equal worth of each individual soul. That doctrine is the heart of Christianity."

Although Helen generally kept her specific religious beliefs to herself, she regarded them as the most important part of her life. "I cannot live without religion," she said. "I could as easily fancy a living body without a heart." In her late forties, she became eager to share her religion with others. *My Religion* was clearly her most direct attempt to do this. It was a 208-page book, published by Doubleday and distributed widely. The book was a powerful and unreserved declaration of her faith in the teachings of Emanuel Swedenborg whose words, she said, were "filled with holy meaning," and "set in my soul" like "jewels bright."

One year later, Helen gave an inspiring address to a national gathering of Swedenborgians in Washington, D.C. In that address, she urged her fellow believers to abandon their sectarian attitude and proclaim the great message that they held in sacred trust:

> I sometimes think that the withdrawing attitude of the New Church keeps people from knowing what a glorious message it has in trust for those who are lost in the fogs of materialism. With all its abounding humanity, Swedenborg's message does not reach the ears of all sorts and conditions of men. If the message does not reach them, it is due not to any narrowness in the Christian ideal which it foreshadows, but to lack of zeal

on the part of those who possess it. I want to see the New Church put on its beautiful garments and shake itself from the dust of aloofness.

"The New Church has a great mission in the world," she said. "The people are in need of just the message that Swedenborg gave for mankind. Instead of merely listening to that message, we should go out and teach it." And she did. Speaking to the people of Scotland, from the pulpit of the New Church in Glasgow, she said that Swedenborg had given her "the golden key to the hidden treasures of the Bible." She added that in Swedenborg's writings she read words that gave her eyes and thoughts that quickened her ear. "As the air is made luminous by the sun, so the Word Ineffable makes bright all darkness."

A LIFE OF SERVICE

As she grew older, Helen's eagerness to share Swedenborg's message took on a different form. Believing that her work for the blind was her special calling, she worked tirelessly—up to eighteen hours a day—carrying on an extensive correspondence, preparing and delivering speeches, and campaigning on behalf of the visually challenged. She traveled the globe six times over, visited dignitaries from every land, and passionately advocated for the sense-deprived. She spoke not only of their plight, but also of their promise and potential. Everywhere she went, whether to Europe, Asia, Australia, or Africa, hospitals and schools for the visually challenged began to spring up, sometimes in the very places where her feet passed.

Helen's activities, in fact, went beyond helping only those who were confronted with blindness and deafness. Advocating for the physically challenged led her to champion social justice on numerous fronts. She spoke against capital punishment. She worked to end ignorance, racism, and poverty. In an era when it was politically incorrect to do so, she upheld the right of workers to strike and the right of women to vote. After touring Hiroshima and Nagasaki, meeting the survivors of the atomic bomb and touching their terrible wounds, she was among the first to campaign against the use of nuclear weapons.

Helen's devotion to the life of useful service, and especially her focus on raising awareness about the needs of the physically challenged, completely occupied her time and energy. Though she remained steadfast in her Swedenborgian faith, she had little time to promote interest in Swedenborg's message. On January 15, 1937—ten years after the publication of *My Religion*—Helen wrote in her journal:

> This morning I received an urgent invitation to attend, in January 1938, a meeting in London to honor Emanuel Swedenborg on the two hundred and fiftieth anniversary of his birth. If it were possible I should accept with greatest pleasure. For Swedenborg's religious writings have brought down to me truths from heaven that have given my spirit a thousand wings to defy the restraints of a sense-deprived body, but I shall not be in England at that time. The claims of the work for the blind are unintermittent, and winter is always the time when demands upon my energies are most urgent.

From 1939 to the time of her death in 1968, Helen said little and wrote little about her religious beliefs, but her actions spoke volumes. While visiting the war-wounded, for example, she did not dispense copies of Swedenborg's religious writings, nor did she attempt to win others over to her faith, but she did incarnate Swedenborg's message in her words and deeds. As she grew older, her profound religious belief and her life of service became increasingly unified and indistinguishable. As she said once after visiting those who had been wounded in World War II, "Often it was not verbal encouragement that was asked of me but a kiss or the laying of my hand on a weary head. This always made me feel as if I were partaking of a sacrament."

Swedenborg wrote in his work *Divine Providence*, paragraph 101, "In the spiritual world, into which everyone comes after death, the question is not asked what your belief has been or your doctrine, but what your life has been . . . for as is known, such as one's life is, such is one's belief." Helen Keller did not wear her religion on her shirtsleeves; it was emblazoned on her heart and incarnated in a life of useful service. Her life had become a living testimony to what had become for her the most important of Swedenborg's religious teachings: "The kingdom of heaven is a kingdom of useful service."

TO LIVE MORE TRULY

Recently, an important letter—written when Helen was eighty years old—has come to light. The letter was written to the Reverend Clayton Priestnal, a New Church minister whom Helen had invited to come to her home for a pastoral visit. During the visit, Helen partook of the sacrament of the Holy Supper. In her letter to the Reverend Priestnal, Helen expresses not only her gratitude for his visit, but also her continuing faith in the teachings of the New Church. The letter is here presented in its entirety:

Arcan Ridge, Westport, Conn.

October 24, 1960

Dear Dr. Priestnal:

I have read your letter to Mrs. Seide with real pleasure and I thank you warmly for all the signs it showed of your thoughtful kindness. Truly it was a joy to me to hear the Communion service from which you read last May, and I shall be delighted to receive a Braille copy from you. There is no inspiration more precious than what comes to me from the New Church. Also, I shall be happy to have the new copy of "The Divine Providence," and every time I touch that glorious work, I shall bless the women whose dear thought conveyed it to me.

It was a happy privilege to have you visit me, and I am grateful to you for speaking so tenderly of our meeting. I have never ceased to miss Mr. Hitz, whom I called "Pflegevater," and I long to communicate with fellow-believers who can inspire me to live more truly as I believe. I felt as though I was in Heaven as I sat with you at the Holy Supper with the sun pouring upon us and the trees and flowers bursting into their glory and the Lord "present with the whole of His redemption." I pray that circumstances may permit us to join now and then in those beautiful experiences of the Spirit. Next month I shall go south to visit my family, but I shall return to Westport in February.

Mrs. Seide joins me in sending affectionate greetings.

Sincerely your friend,

Life is either a daring adventure or it is nothing.

The words, "and the Lord present in the whole of His redemption" is a direct quotation from Swedenborg's final work, *True Christian Religion*, paragraph 716. This is the last written statement that we have in which Helen discusses her religion. One year later, in October 1961, Helen suffered a stroke and was forced to retire from public service. She died on June 1, 1968, at the age of eighty-eight.

AN UNCONQUERABLE FAITH

Although Helen Keller remained faithful to the teachings of Emanuel Swedenborg throughout her life, she never chose to separate herself from her brothers and sisters in other religions. She remained a champion for all those who were sincere in their beliefs and who struggled for the spiritual and physical liberation of mankind. In a strong letter to a nun who had tried to persuade Helen to embrace the Catholic faith, Helen wrote:

> I have an unconquerable faith in the sincerity and goodness of many friends who hold opinions quite different from mine and yours, and if they are found to be wicked, as Cardinal Gibbons declares people to be who will not listen to the Church, let me share their fate rather than be false and unloving.

In 1929, after a public speech in which she had expressed enthusiasm for the teachings of Baha Ullah, the *New York World* reported that Helen had become a follower of the Baha'i religion. In a private letter to the Reverend Paul Sperry (a New Church minister), Helen expressed her dismay over the newspaper article, and asked him to help her correct the misunderstanding. In her letter to the Reverend Sperry, she wrote:

It is important to me that I should not be misrepresented in my religion. As you know, since I was sixteen years old, I have been a strong believer in the doctrines of Emanuel Swedenborg. Why should I change my faith, since it opens my eyes to all that is beautiful and noble in the thoughts and beliefs of men and makes my dark silent world sweet and livable? I have a profound respect for the teachings of Baha Ullah, just as I have for the noble thoughts of all great prophets and seers. But it never occurred to me that anyone would think that I had "adopted the Persian religion" because I was speaking to Bahai followers.

Helen indeed honored all who honored the spirit of God as it was manifested in the lives of all people, in all religions. But her faith in the New Church remained steadfast. In her last published work, *Teacher* (1955), Helen spoke of her undimmed enthusiasm for Swedenborg's teachings. Quoting Walt Whitman she writes:

O Spirit, as a runner strips,
Upon a windy afternoon,
Be unencumbered of what troubles you—
Arise with grace
And greatly go, with the wind upon your face.

She then adds, "In that state of exhilaration I had accepted the teachings of Emanuel Swedenborg, had drunk in his interpretation of the Bible, fearless, reverent, yet as unconfined as the sun, the clouds, the sea."

Helen Keller's religious faith was based on Swedenborg's teachings, to be sure, but it was as "unconfined as the sun, the clouds, the sea." Her Lord was Jesus Christ, but this Christ was not the narrow God of a sectarian Christianity. In him, she saw the smiling God of all souls, encompassing multitudes in every faith, and showering all with unceasing love, wisdom, and power for useful service. Helen Keller knew that God's true church—the Kingdom of Heaven—is not here or there, but rather, within each person. And that is why she could rise above all theological language and religious definitions to proclaim:

> I believe that life is given us so that we may grow in love,
> And I believe that God is in me
> As the sun is in the color and fragrance of the flower
> The Light in my darkness,
> The Voice in my silence.

EDITOR'S NOTE

Light in My Darkness IS A REVISION OF *My Religion*, A BOOK ORIGI-
nally published in 1927, when Helen Keller was forty-seven years
old. Many who have read the earlier edition have been powerfully
touched by the beauty and power of her words. Yet extraordinary
as *My Religion* was then and remains today, it lacks organization
and structure. It is like a gathering of stars randomly scattered
through a dark sky: here and there the reader may identify a con-
stellation, but as Helen herself admitted, there is little order.

In a letter to a Swedenborgian minister, the Reverend Paul
Sperry, Helen explained how difficult it is for a blind person to
write a book:

> I find writing a book a hard task. It is difficult for me
> as a blind person to handle a mass of material with
> skill because I cannot go over my manuscript often or
> quickly. I write several hours a day and then have to
> go to South Orange or Briarcliff or somewhere else
> to lecture. When I get back to my typewriter, I have
> lost the thread of my discourse. Having someone read
> to me what I have written would take too long; so I

simply start it again, hit or miss. When more of the manuscript is ready, I shall want to send it to you, if you will be so kind as to read it and criticize it severely and perhaps rearrange it to improve the construction. . . . *Construction is not one of my strong points* [emphasis added].

In his response to this letter, Sperry told Helen to keep writing and leave the matter of arrangement and construction for later, when editorial assistance would be provided. But the much-needed assistance never came. A project so religious in nature had little appeal for Helen's editorial assistant at Doubleday, and even less for Anne Sullivan Macy. Nearing the end of her labors, Helen lamented, "So far not a single page has been revised, or for that matter read to me." She vividly described her feelings about the state of the work in a letter to Sperry:

I am wandering forlornly in the Valley of Despond. There is something weighing me down to earth. It should be a book, but it is not. It is only the faintest resemblance of a book. Indeed, the resemblance is so slight that I doubt it would occur to anybody but myself to notice it. Mrs. Macy keeps insisting that I should send this undisciplined offspring of my brain to you as it is, "without one plea." But I am fearful that you would not see anything in it.

One month later she did send off the manuscript to Sperry, though "with fear and trembling and blushing misgivings." But Sperry did not share Helen's fear; nor did he understand her misgivings. In fact, he was delighted with the work, and with good reason. The love and genius manifested in it covered a multitude of imperfections. Sperry's opinion was that the book was "spontaneous, unlabored, fresh. . . . just what we want." When he introduced the book to the public, he offered this assessment, which perhaps reveals more about his own intentions than Helen's: "*My Religion* is not a literary production prepared for publication; it is a public profession of faith, a spontaneous utterance of the heart, a grateful tribute to Swedenborg."

The value of the book was not lost on the public. *My Religion* sold remarkably well in 1927 and has remained in print ever since. The author, however, still had misgivings. When she was at last able to read a copy in Braille, she said, "I am particularly chagrined over the construction, which seems to me dismally chaotic." The combination of indifference among those who worked most closely with her and the urgency of those who were eager to bring the book to the public had prevented *My Religion* from achieving the excellence she had set for it. This new edition, then, is offered in the hope of fulfilling Helen Keller's wishes—providing her with the editorial assistance she sought but did not receive.

THE EDITORIAL CHANGES

Helen Keller is a prose poet, writing in bursts of radiant light. Many of the passages that appeared in *My Religion* were written at various times in her life—some as early as 1903—and pasted into the manuscript as Helen composed it in the late 1920s. In some cases this technique led to severe fragmentation of the text. To resolve this difficulty, in this edition passages that were only loosely strung together have been rearranged and placed in more coherent patterns. The eight unwieldy sections of the first edition have been reordered into twelve distinct chapters with subheadings to clarify their contents. Furthermore, materials not present in the first edition have been added to elucidate and expand the original text. A complete list of the sources follows.

Other revisions include modernization of several words and phrases, substitution of inclusive language where appropriate, correction of spelling and typographical errors, alteration of punctuation to conform to current standards, and emendation of a few historical inaccuracies. Extra paragraph breaks have been added and a very few passages that distracted from the main message have been delicately pruned. It must be emphasized, however, that these revisions are negligible next to all that has been retained.

The materials in chapters 1–12 and in the epilogue are gathered from the following sources:

1. Awakenings

• Picture caption: Helen Keller, *My Religion* (New York: Swedenborg Foundation, 1986), 153–154.

• *My Religion*, 29–30, 154, 30, 152, 153, 150, 153–154, 150, 36–49.

• "Helen Keller and the New Church," by Paul Sperry. *The Messenger*, vol. 133:19, (November 9, 1927): 336–339. Sperry's article contains excerpts from an introduction that Helen wrote for a two-volume collection of extracts from Swedenborg's writings (in Braille), in 1911. It also contains extracts from several letters that Helen wrote to Sperry in 1926 and 1927 while she was writing *My Religion*.

• "Helen Keller in Scotland," *Swedenborg Society Magazine* (Spring 1993). The article is excerpted from the book *Helen in Scotland* (London: Methuen and Company, 1933). It contains an address given to the New Church of Scotland in Glasgow on June 22, 1932.

2. Swedenborg's Search

- Picture caption: *My Religion*, 33.
- *My Religion*, 17–20.
- *My Religion*, 21–22.
- *My Religion*, 23–29.
- *My Religion*, 30–33.
- Sperry, 337.
- *My Religion*, 34.
- Sperry, 337.

3. Swedenborg's Accomplishments

- Picture caption: *My Religion*, 62.
- *My Religion*, 50–57, 61–66.

4. Into the Holy of Holies

- Picture caption: *My Religion*, 70.
- *My Religion*, 69–91.

5. Revolutionary Ideas

- Picture caption: *My Religion*, 99.
- Helen Keller, "How I Would Help the World," introduction to Emanuel Swedenborg, *True Christian Religion*, edited by Ernest Rhys (New York: E. P. Dutton/Everyman's Library, 1933). This essay has been reprinted as a pamphlet entitled *How I Would Help the World* (Bryn Athyn, Pennsylvania: General Church Press, 1980). The material used in this chapter is taken from page 6 of the pamphlet.
- *My Religion*, 95–98, 82–84, 136–138, 46, 99, 118–121, 139–141.

6. Secrets of the Spiritual World

- Picture caption: *My Religion*, 104.
- *My Religion*, 85, 102–106, 108, 107, 99–101, 117, 155–156.

7. The Gospel of Love

- Picture caption: Sperry, 337.

- *My Religion*, 114–118. Note: On page 118, Helen writes, "Thus at last a faint ray, travelling through infinity from the Divine Soul, reached the mind of the deaf, blind humanity, and lo, the second coming of the Lord was *at hand*" (emphasis added). Six years later, in her introduction to the Everyman edition of *True Christian Religion* (1933), Helen writes, "Thus at last a faint ray, travelling through infinity from the Divine Soul, reached the mind of deaf, blind humanity, and lo, the second coming of the Lord was *an accomplished fact*" (*How I Would Help the World*, 9; emphasis added).
- *My Religion*, 121–126.
- Sperry, 337.
- Helen Keller, "A Vision of Service," an address delivered at the Assembly of the General Convention of Swedenborgian Churches, Washington, D.C., May 14, 1928. Reprinted in *The Messenger* 134: 445–446; and in *New Church Life* (October, 1980): 444–448.

8. The Gospel of Joy
- Picture caption: *My Religion*, 133.
- *My Religion*, 130–136.

9. Overcoming
- Picture caption: *My Religion*, 146.
- *My Religion*, 144–148, 112–113.

10. The Mystic Sense
- Picture caption: *My Religion*, 111.
- *My Religion*, 86–87, 148–151, 154–155, 110–112, 157, 109–110.
- Helen Keller, *The Open Door* (New York: Doubleday, 1957), 139.
- *My Religion*, 156–157, 34–35.

11. The Great Message
- Picture caption: *How I Would Help the World*, 1.
- *My Religion*, 34.

- *How I Would Help the World*, 2, 1–4.
- *My Religion*, 122, 50, 92–94.
- *How I Would Help the World*, 1–3, 9.

12. My Luminous Universe

- Picture caption: *My Religion*, 35.
- Helen Keller, "My Luminous Universe," *Guideposts* (June 1956); rept. March 1995, 17–20. This essay was originally published when Helen was 76 years old. In reprinting it in its fiftieth-anniversary issue of March 1995, the editorial staff of *Guideposts* magazine prefaced it with the following: "Our articles present tested methods for developing courage, strength and positive attitudes through faith in God. Perhaps no article better illustrates these precepts than this extraordinary tribute to God's power by one of the most memorable and beloved personalities of the twentieth century." This article is reprinted with permission from *Guideposts* magazine. Copyright © 1956 by Guideposts, Carmel, New York 10512.

Epilogue

- Picture caption: Dennis Wepman, *American Women of Achievement* (Philadelphia: Chelsea House, 1987), 83.
- "A Vision of Service," 446–447.
- Helen Keller, *Helen Keller's Journal* (New York: Doubleday, 1938), 117.
- Letter to the Reverend Clayton Priestnal from Helen Keller, October 24, 1960. Courtesy Carroll Odhner, director of the Swedenborg Library, Academy of the New Church, Bryn Athyn, Pennsylvania.
- Joseph Lash, *Helen and Teacher* (New York: Delacourt Press, 1980), 430, 557, 786.
- Helen Keller, *Teacher: Anne Sullivan Macy* (New York: Doubleday, 1955), 179. See also p. 139 where Helen writes, "I accepted the beliefs of the New Church joyously and not on account of the 'consolation' they afforded me for deafness or blindness or any other difficulty."
- Helen Keller, *The Open Door*, 138–139.

The following works by Emanuel Swedenborg were cited by Helen Keller in this book. All are published by the Swedenborg Foundation, West Chester, Pennsylvania.

Arcana Coelestia, 12 volumes
Divine Love and Wisdom
Divine Providence
Heaven and Hell
True Christian Religion, 2 volumes

Also cited by Keller was:

Tafel, Rudolf, L., ed. *Documents concerning the life and character of Emanuel Swedenborg*. London: Swedenborg Society, Vol. I, 1875; Vol. II, in two parts, 1877.

— RAY SILVERMAN
Huntingdon Valley, Pennsylvania

FOR FURTHER READING

Other related works by Helen Keller include:

Helen in Scotland. London: Methuen and Company, 1933.
Helen Keller's Journal. New York: Doubleday, 1938.
Let Us Have Faith. New York: Doubleday, 1941.
The Open Door. New York: Doubleday, 1957.
The Story of My Life. New York: Andor, 1976.
Teacher: Anne Sullivan Macy. New York: Doubleday, 1955.

Excellent treatments of Helen Keller's life and accomplishments include:

Brooks, Van Wyck. Helen Keller: Sketch for a Portrait. New York: E. P. Dutton and Company, 1956.

Gibson, William. The Miracle Worker: A Play for Television. New York: Alfred Knopf, 1957.

Harrity, Richard, and Ralph G. Martin. The Three Lives of Helen Keller. New York: Doubleday, 1962.

Herrmann, Dorothy. Helen Keller: A Life. New York: Knopf, 1998.

Lash, Joseph. Helen and Teacher: The Story of Helen Keller and Anne Sullivan Macy. New York: Delacourt Press/Seymour Lawrence, 1980.

The following books are particularly useful for younger readers:

Benjamin, Anne. *Young Helen Keller: Woman of Courage.* New York: Troll Associates, 1992.

Kudlinski, Kathleen V. *Helen Keller: A Light for the Blind.* New York: Viking Kestrel, 1989.

Peare, Catherine O. *The Helen Keller Story.* New York: Thomas Y. Crowell, 1959.

Wepman, Dennis. *Helen Keller: Humanitarian.* New York: Chelsea House, 1987.

The New Century Edition of the Works of Emanuel Swedenborg (NCE) available through the Swedenborg Foundation include:

Divine Love and Wisdom
Divine Providence
Heaven and Hell
Life / Faith
The Lord
New Jerusalem
Sacred Scripture / White Horse
Secrets of Heaven
True Christianity

INDEX

About the Editor

Ray Silverman is the author of *Rise Above It: Spiritual Development through the Ten Commandments* (co-authored with his wife, Star). More recently, he has authored *The Core of Johnny Appleseed* and the introduction for the stand-alone edition of Helen Keller's inspirational essay *How I Would Help the World*. Ray holds a PhD from the University of Michigan, an MAT from Wesleyan University, and an MDiv from the Academy of the New Church Theological School. He currently serves as associate professor of religion, English, and moral philosophy at Bryn Athyn College.